RECORDED VERSIONS
GUITAR

AUTHENTIC TRANSCRIPTIONS
WITH NOTES AND TABLATURE

SCOTT HENDERSON
BLUES GUITAR COLLECTION

Photos courtesy of Scott Henderson

Music transcriptions by Addi Booth

ISBN 978-1-4234-1227-4

HAL•LEONARD®
CORPORATION

7777 W. BLUEMOUND RD. P.O. BOX 13819 MILWAUKEE, WI 53213

In Australia Contact:
Hal Leonard Australia Pty. Ltd.
4 Lentara Court
Cheltenham, Victoria, 3192 Australia
Email: ausadmin@halleonard.com.au

Visit Hal Leonard Online at
www.halleonard.com

from *Well to the Bone*
Ashes
Written by Scott Henderson

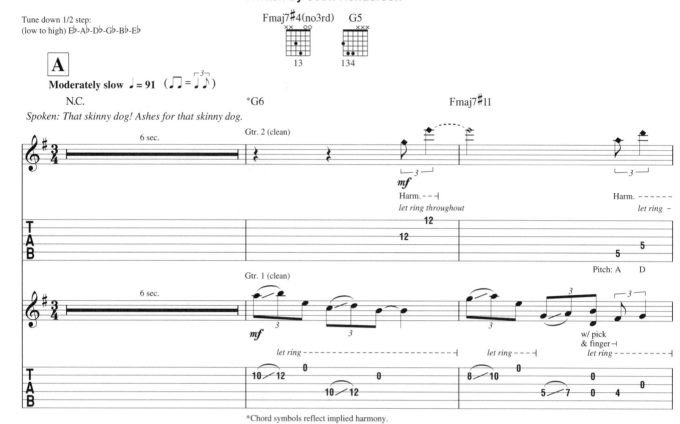

*Chord symbols reflect implied harmony.

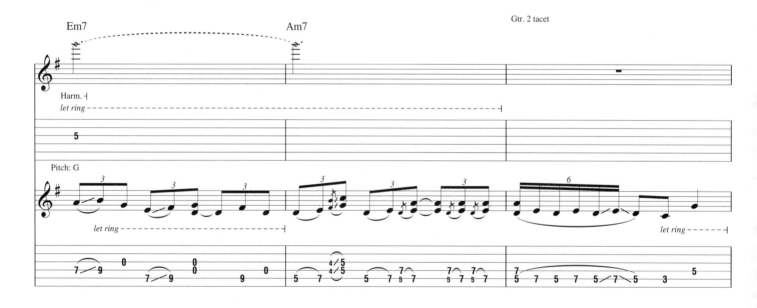

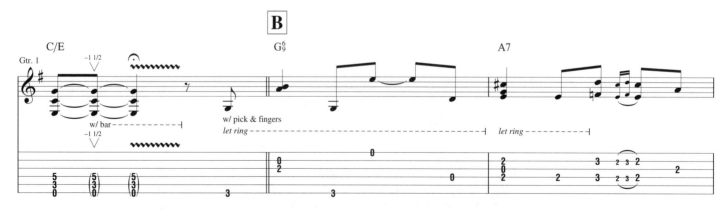

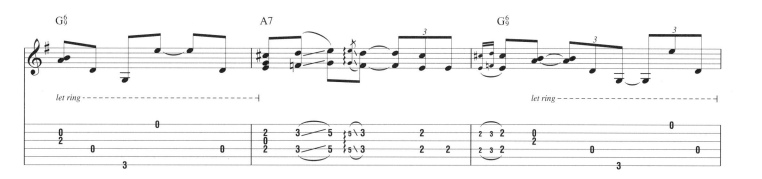

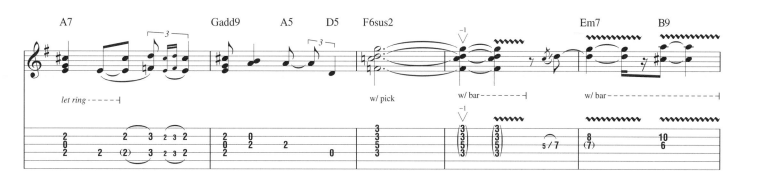

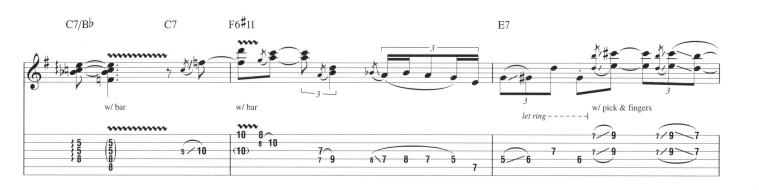

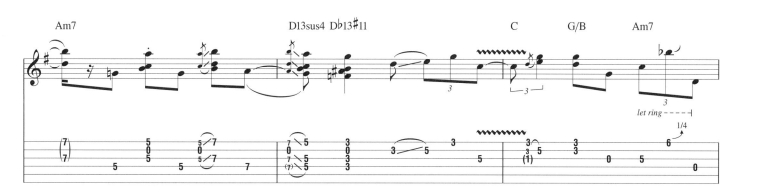

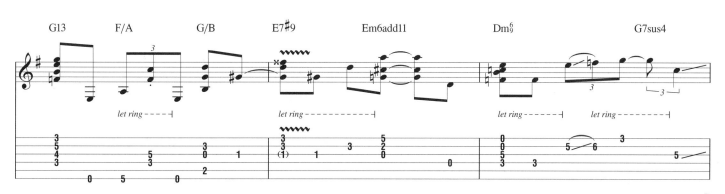

*Played as straight eighth-notes.

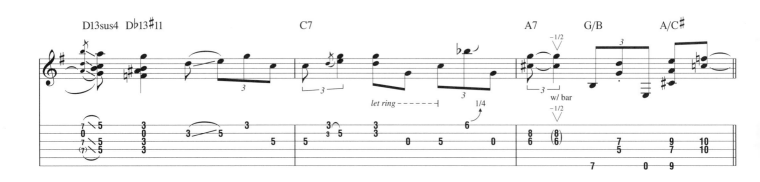

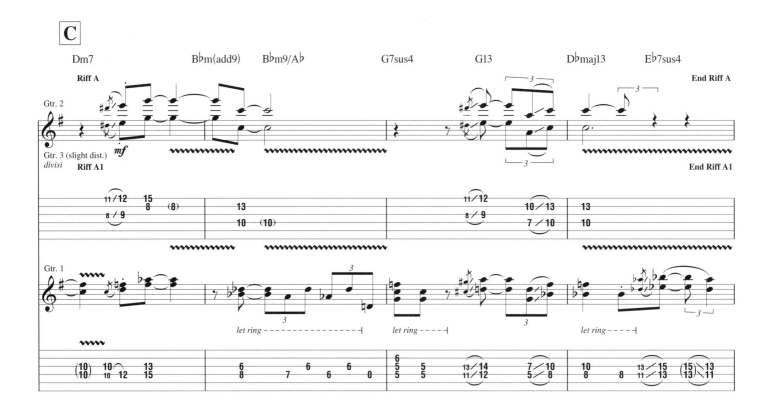

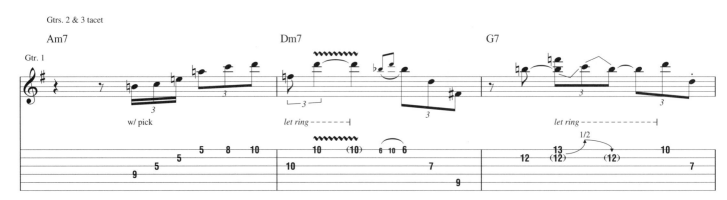

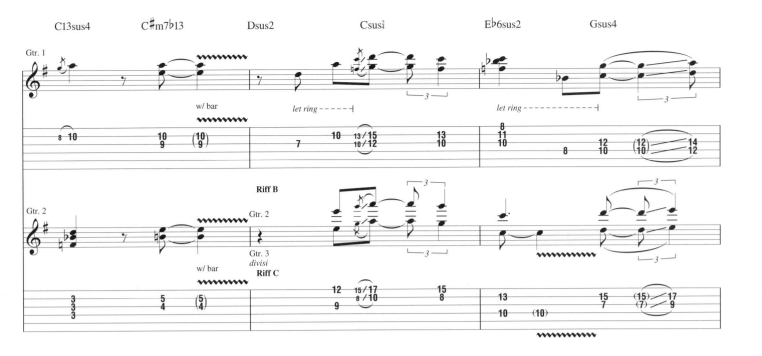

**Played as straight eighth-notes.

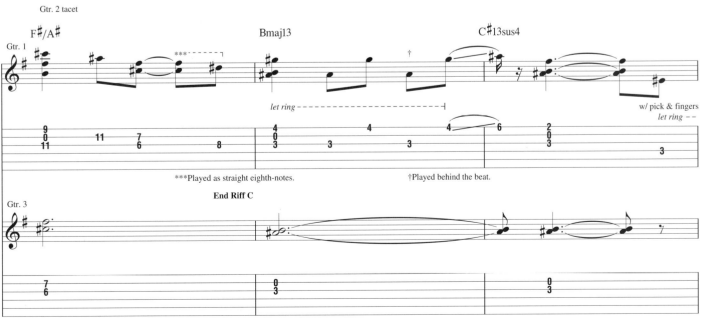

***Played as straight eighth-notes.   †Played behind the beat.

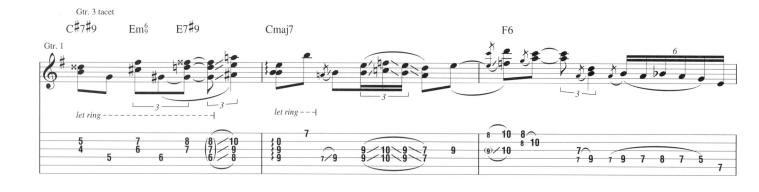

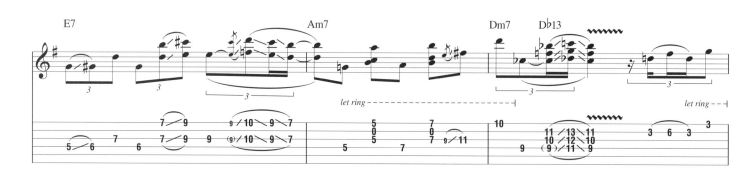

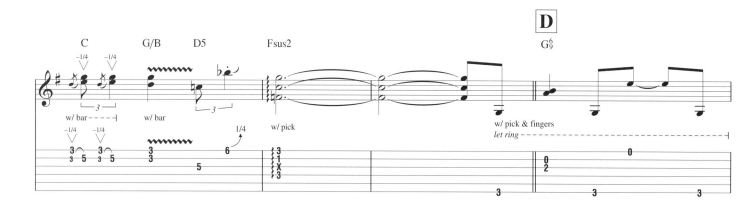

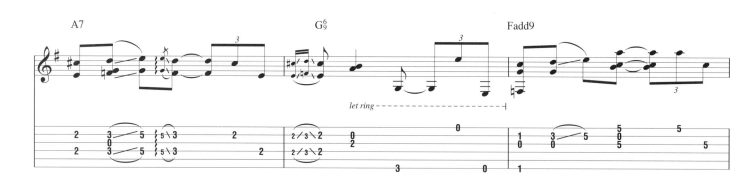

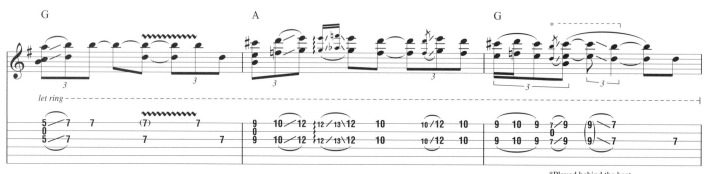

*Played behind the beat.

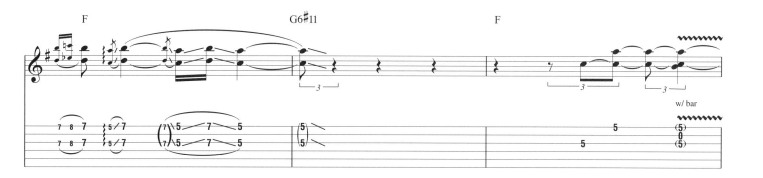

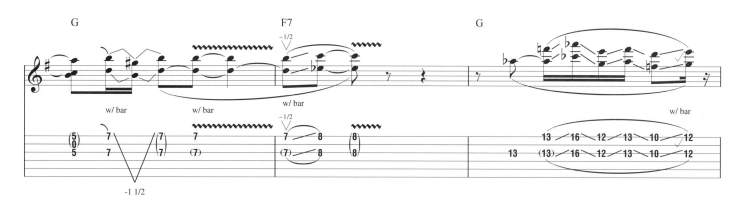

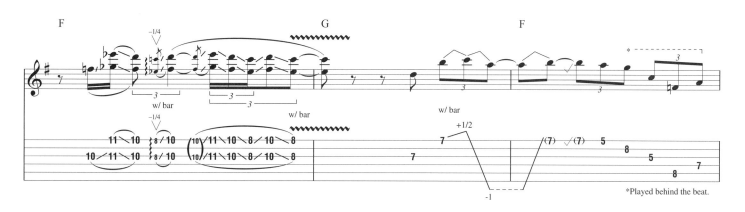

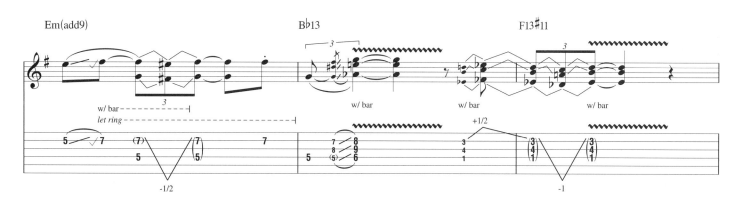

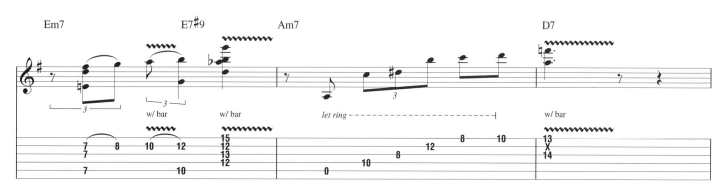

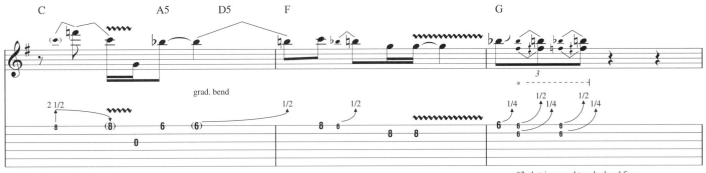

*2nd string caught under bend finger.

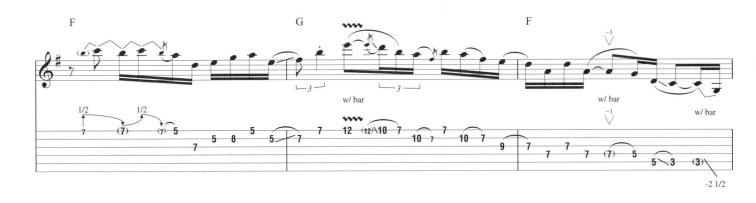

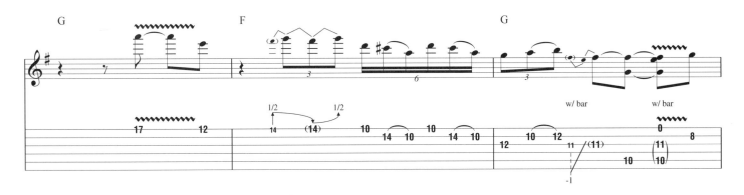

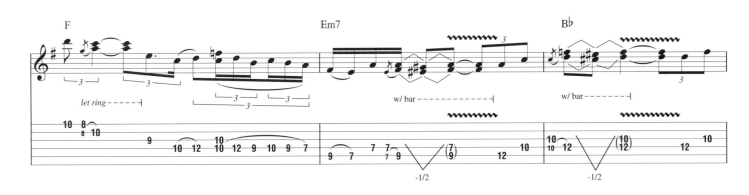

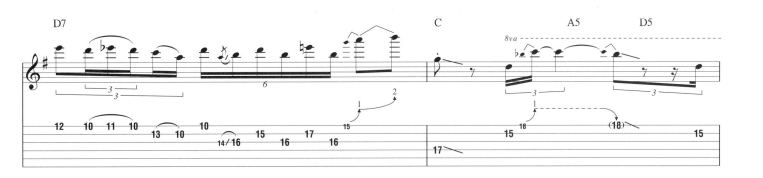

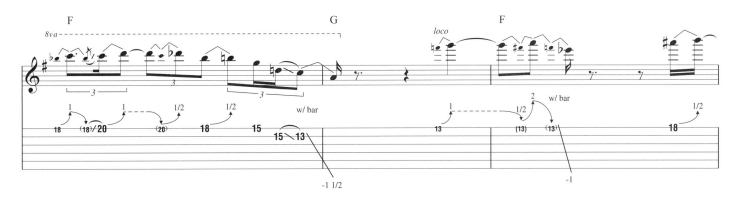

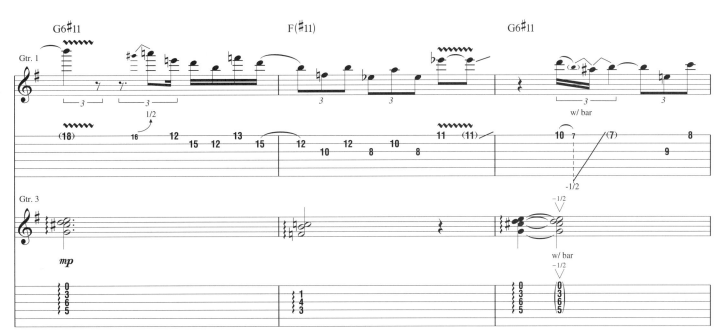

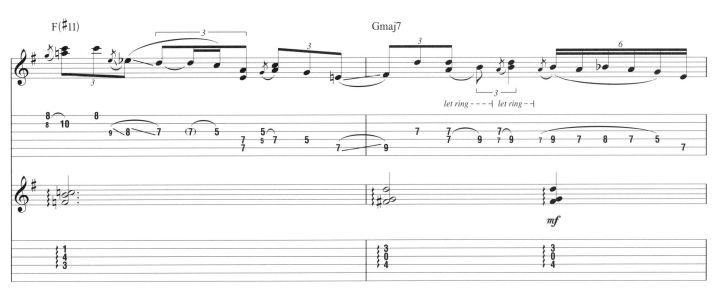

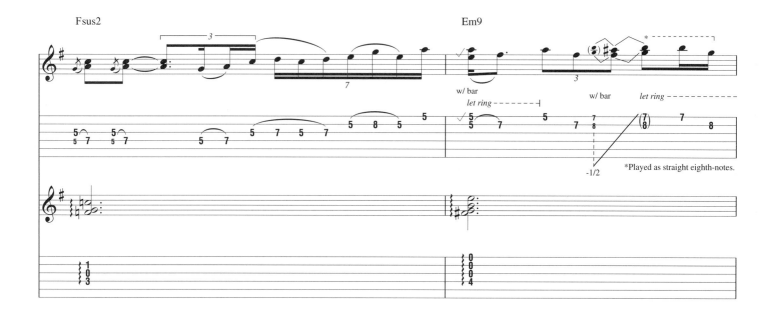

*Played as straight eighth-notes.

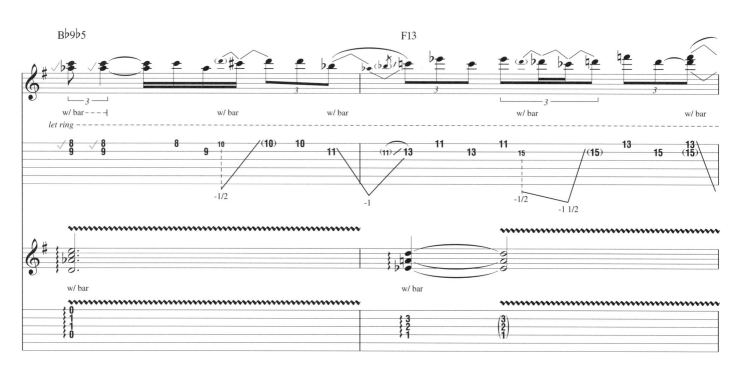

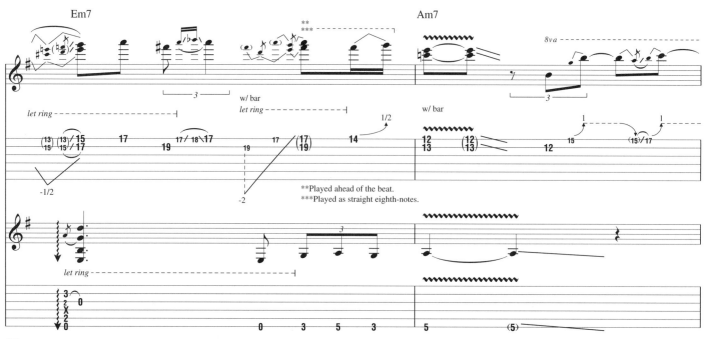

**Played ahead of the beat.
***Played as straight eighth-notes.

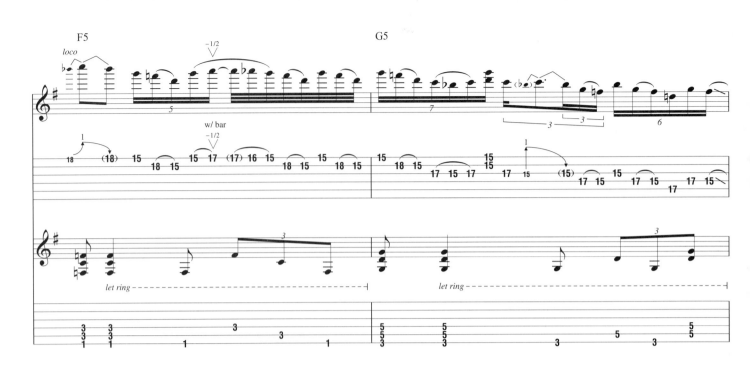

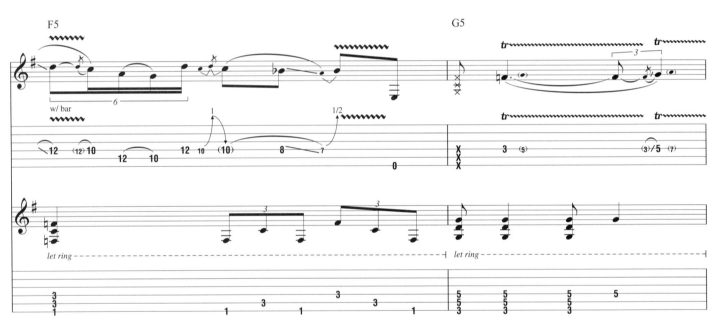

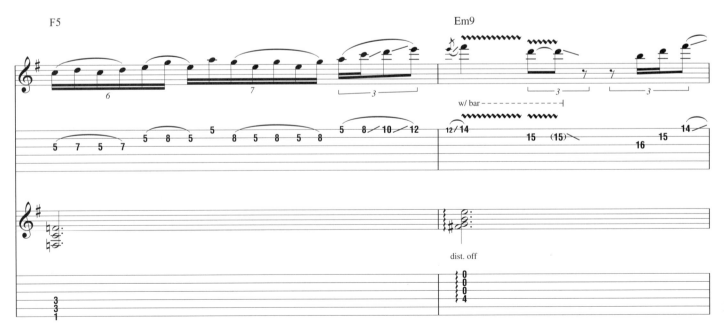

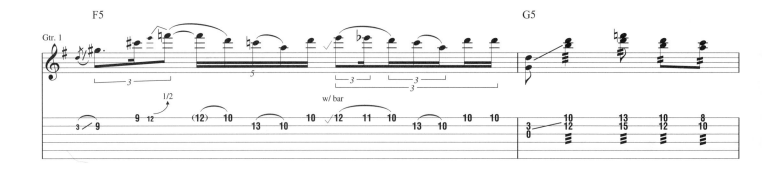

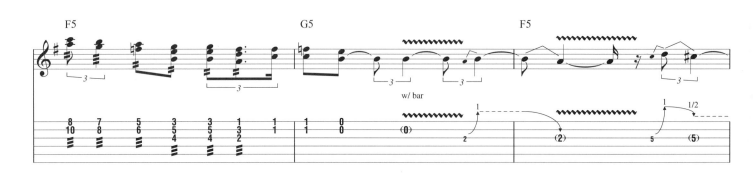

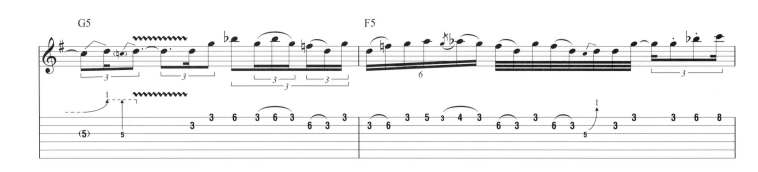

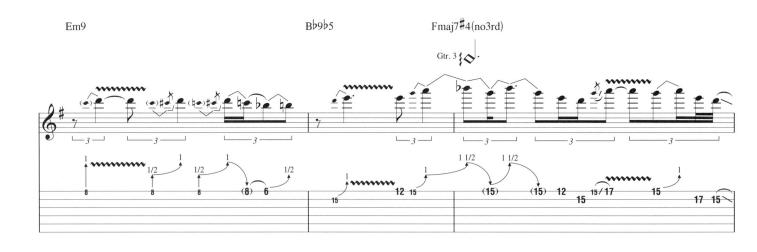

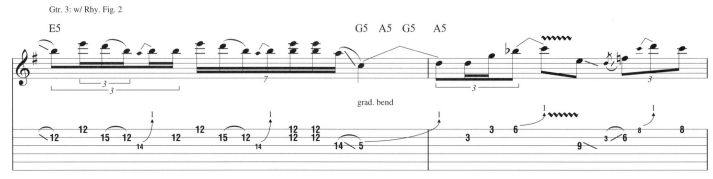

16

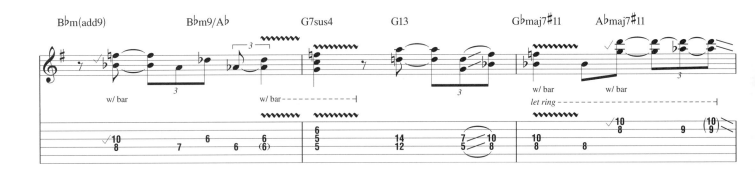

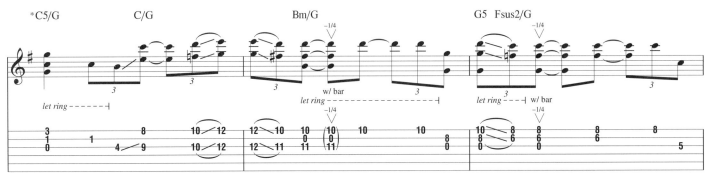

*Bass plays G pedal, next 3 meas.

Gtr. 2: w/ Riff B
Gtr. 3: w/ Riff C

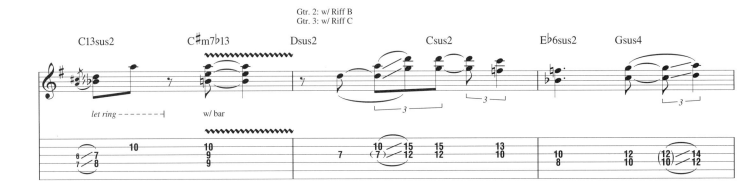

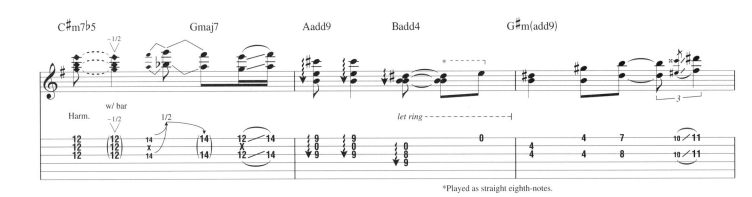

*Played as straight eighth-notes.

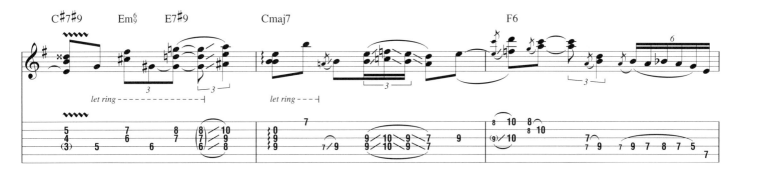

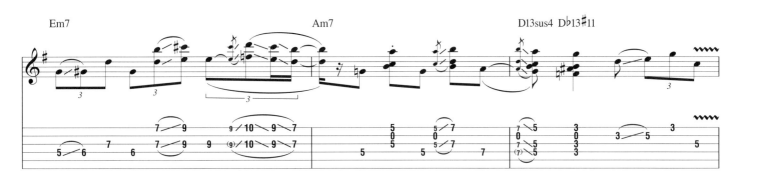

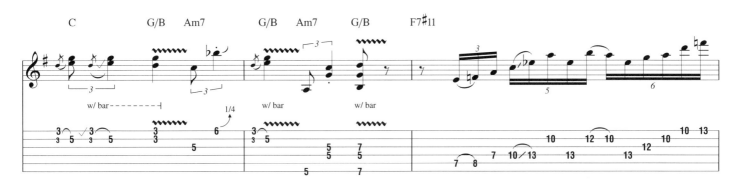

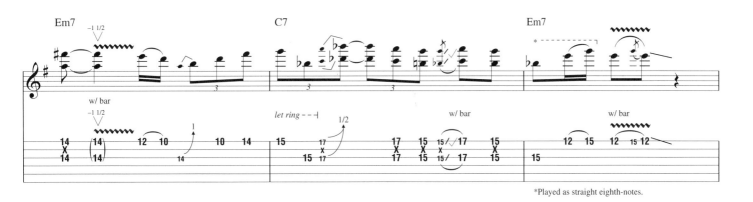

*Played as straight eighth-notes.

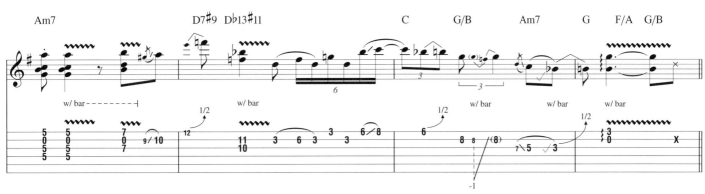

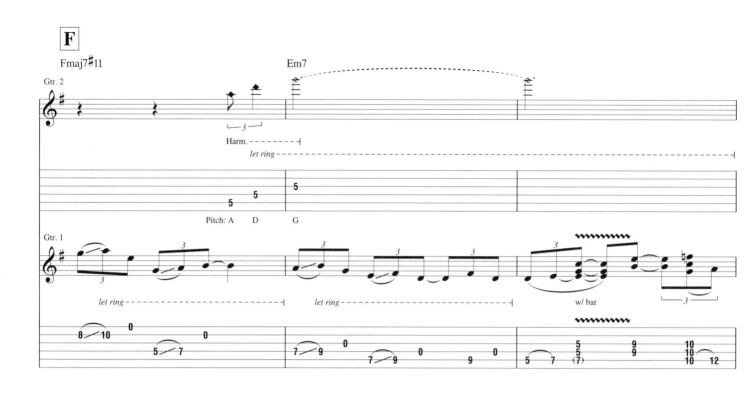

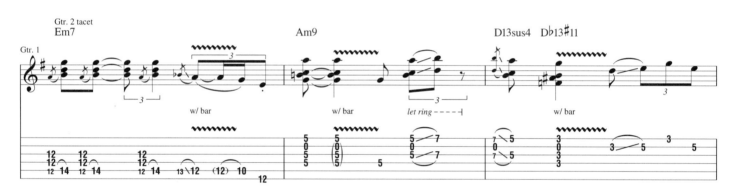

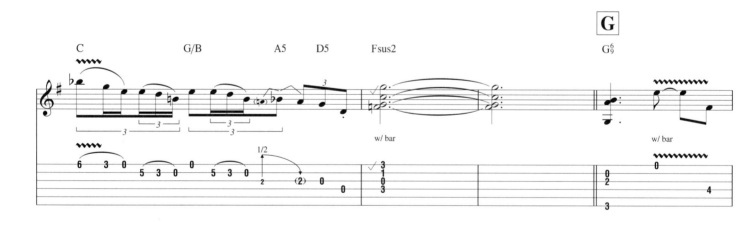

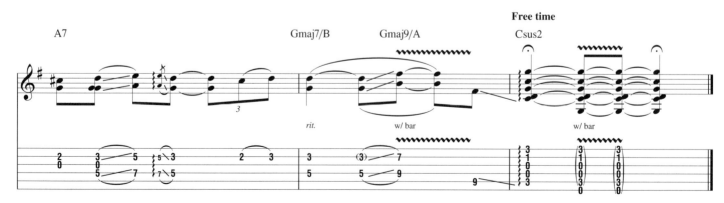

from *Dog Party*

Dog Party

Written by Scott Henderson

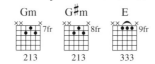

Tune down 1/2 step:
(low to high) E♭-A♭-D♭-G♭-B♭-E♭

Intro
Moderately ♩ = 118

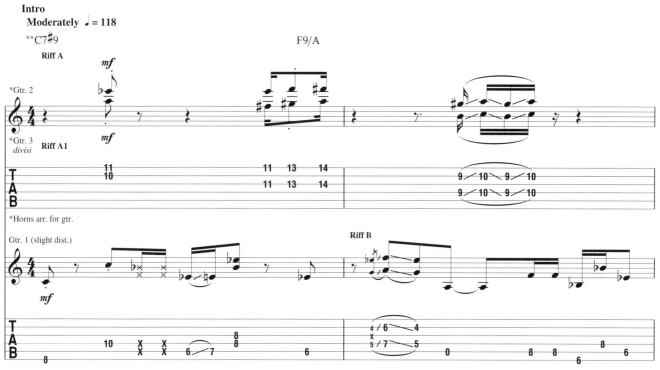

*Horns arr. for gtr.

**Chord symbols reflect overall harmony.

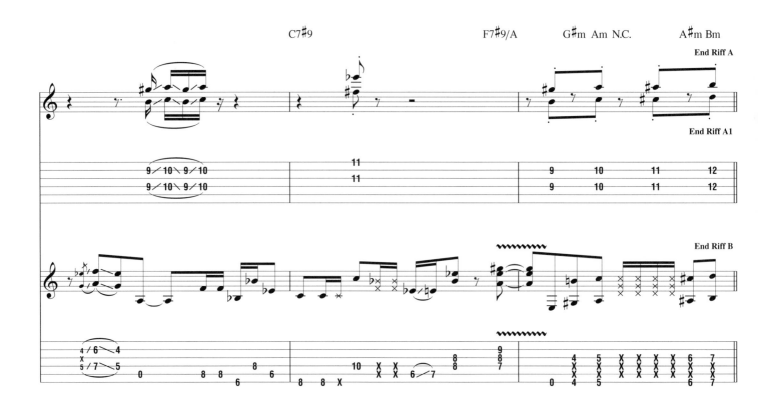

Verse

Gtrs. 2 & 3 tacet

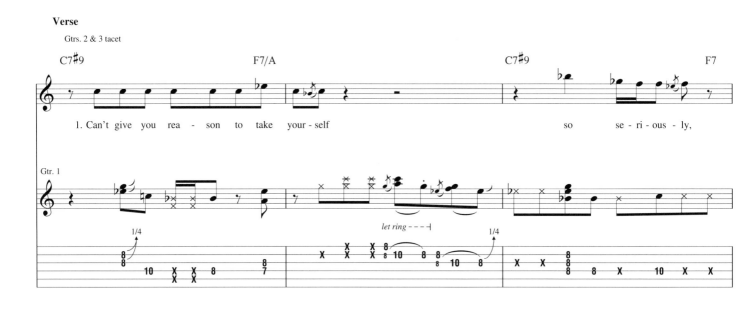

1. Can't give you rea - son to take your - self so se - ri - ous - ly,

Gtr. 1

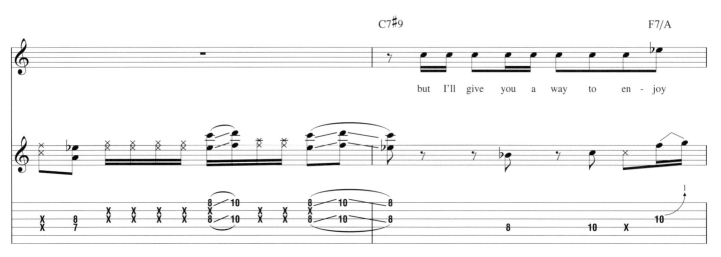

but I'll give you a way to en - joy

your - self.

Come on o - ver here with __ me. __

You say you don't wan - na leave your house

feel - ing sad and blue.

Here's a rea - son to change __ your __ mind. __

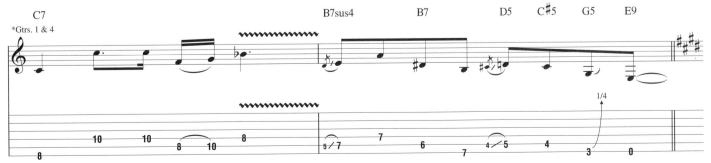

*Gtrs. 1 & 4

*Gtr. 4 (slight dist.), played *mf*.
Composite arrangement

%‌ **Chorus**

3rd time, Gtrs. 2 & 3 tacet

Gtr. 4 tacet

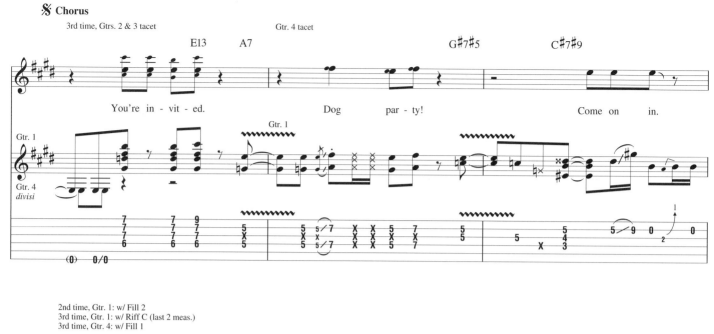

You're in - vit - ed.   Dog   par - ty!   Come on   in.

2nd time, Gtr. 1: w/ Fill 2
3rd time, Gtr. 1: w/ Riff C (last 2 meas.)
3rd time, Gtr. 4: w/ Fill 1

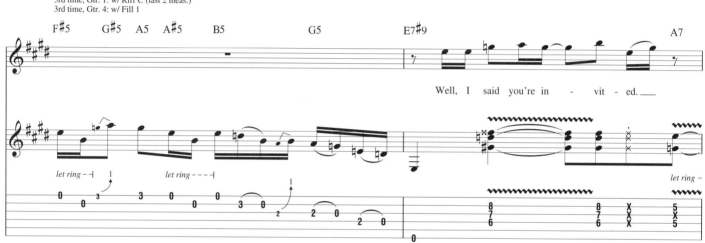

Well, I   said you're in - vit - ed. ___

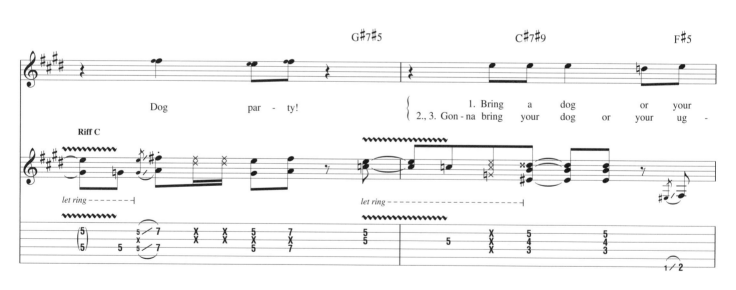

Dog   par - ty!   1. Bring   a   dog   or   your
2., 3. Gon - na bring   your   dog   or   your   ug -

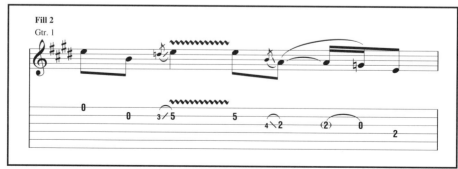

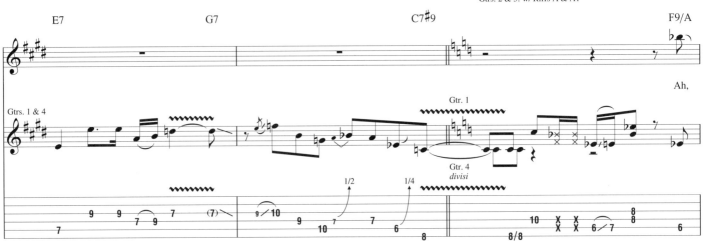

Verse

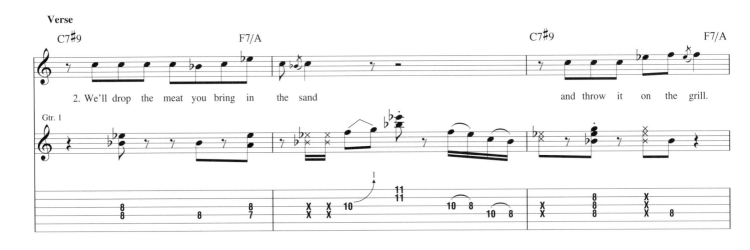

26

but I think your sis - ter will.

I got a stud who wants __ to meet your bitch   if na - ture has its way.

It __ don't mean __ we're re - lat - ed,   no, __   no,   no. __

*Sung ahead of the beat.

D.S. al Coda 1

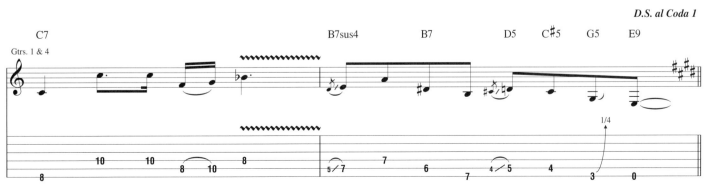

Coda 1

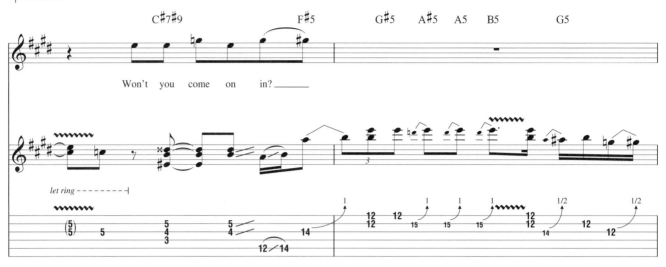

Guitar Solo

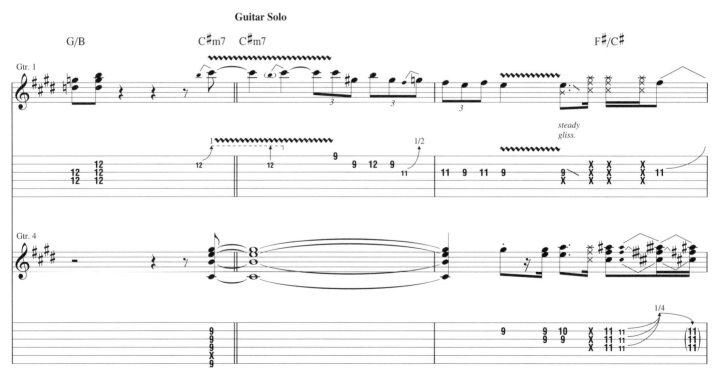

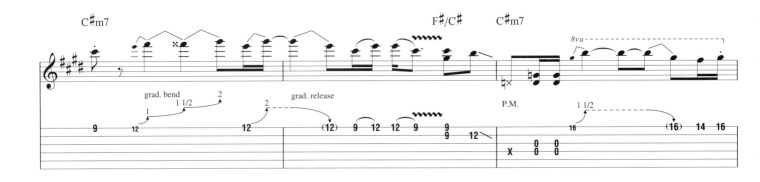

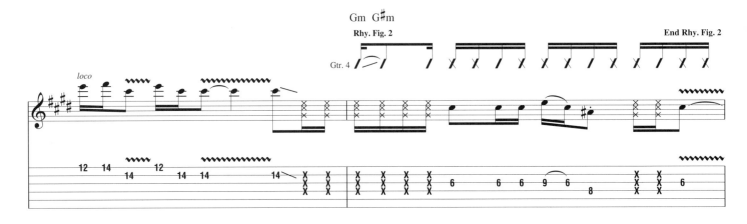

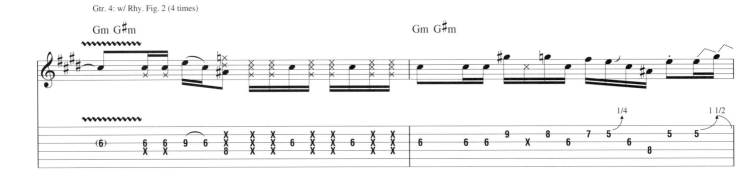

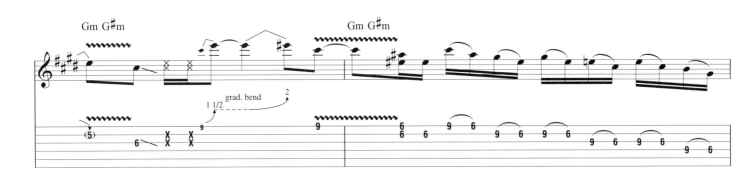

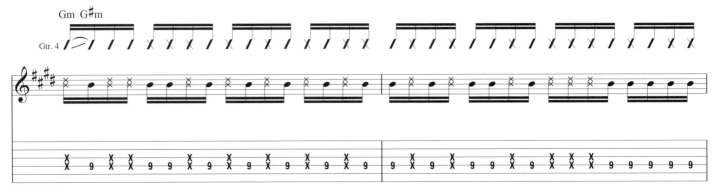

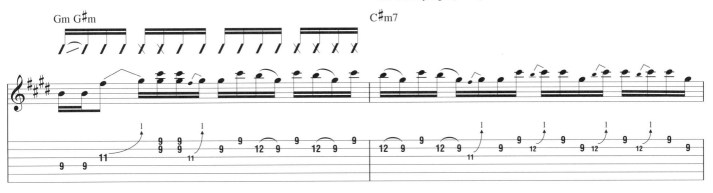

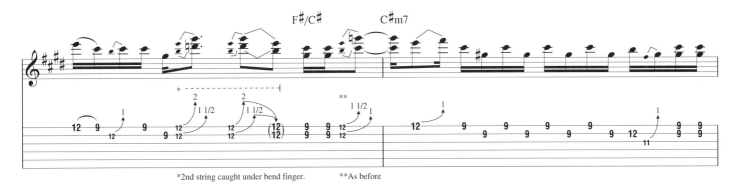

*2nd string caught under bend finger.   **As before

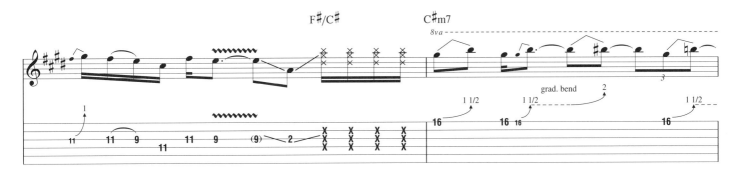

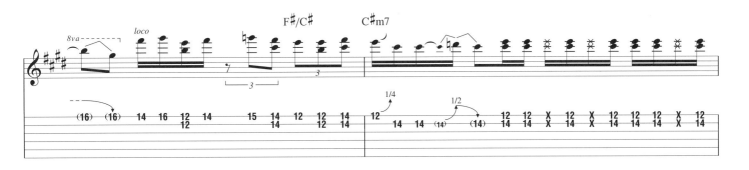

Breakdown

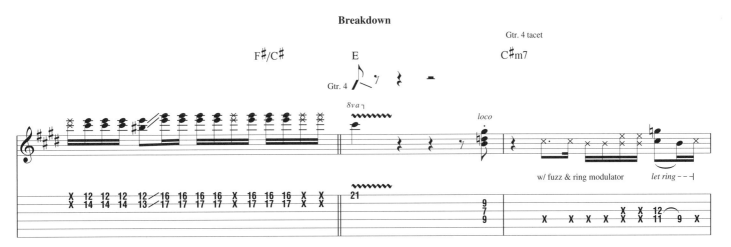

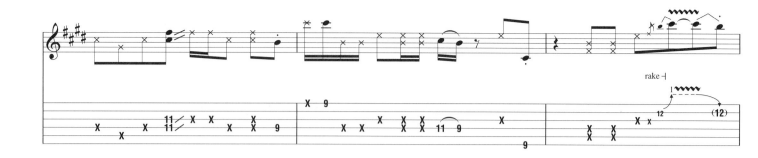

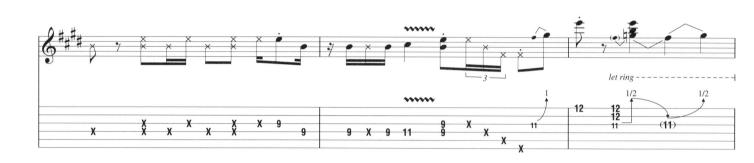

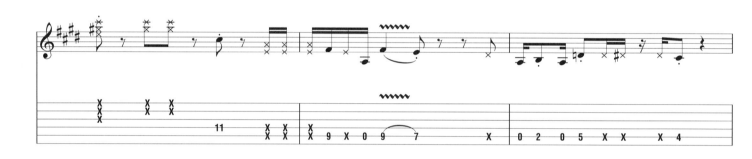

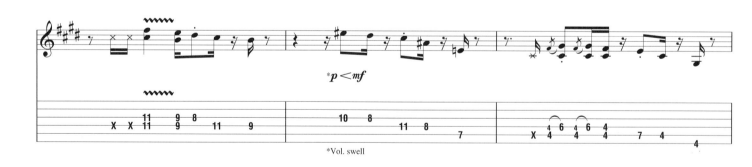

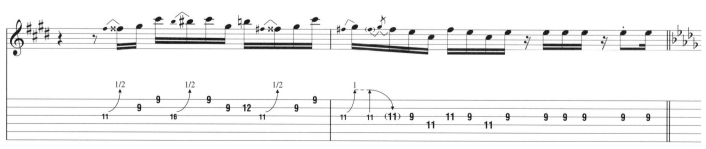

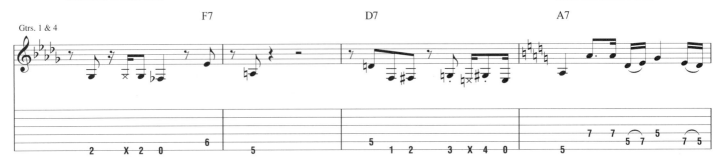

D.S. al Coda 2

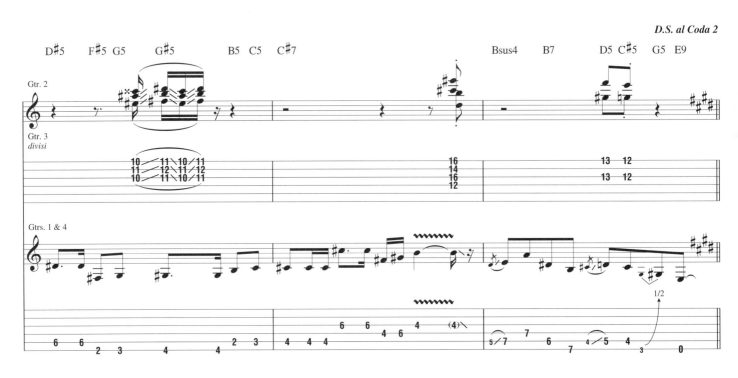

⊕ Coda 2

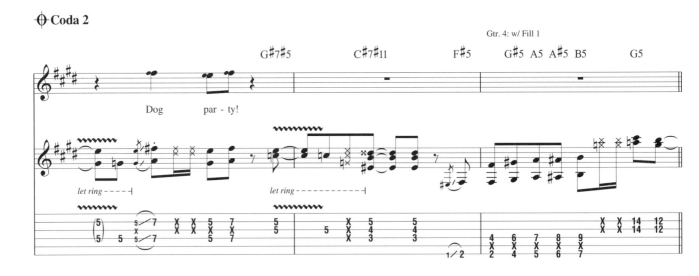

Outro-Guitar Solo

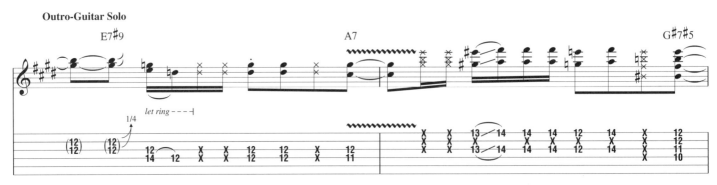

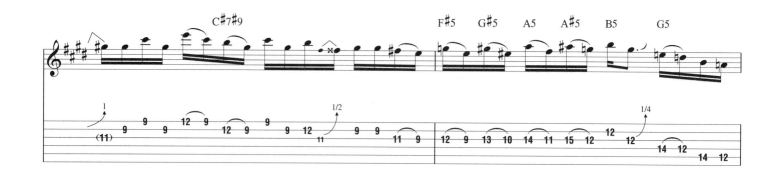

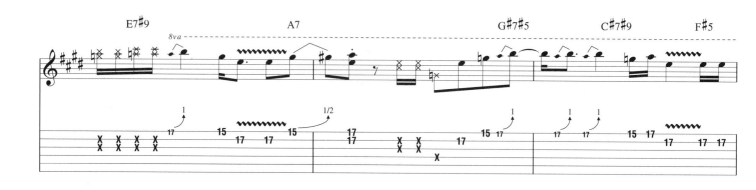

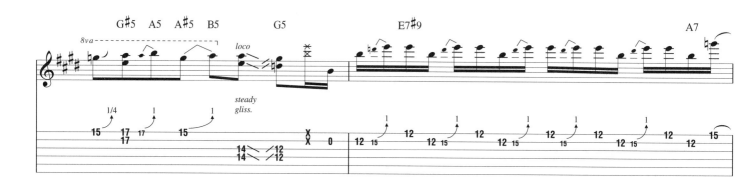

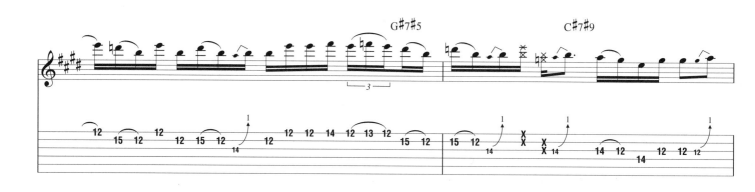

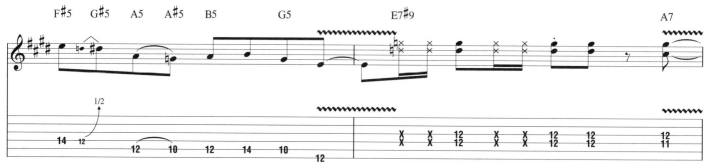

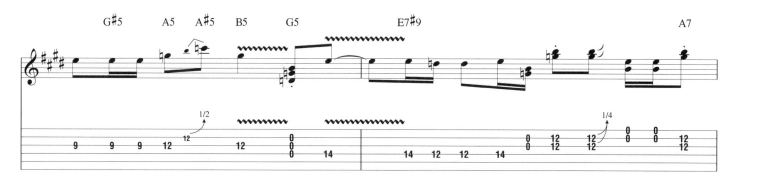

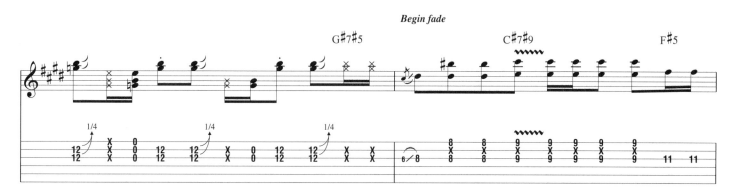

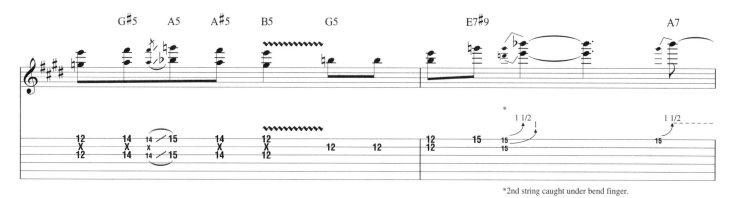

*2nd string caught under bend finger.

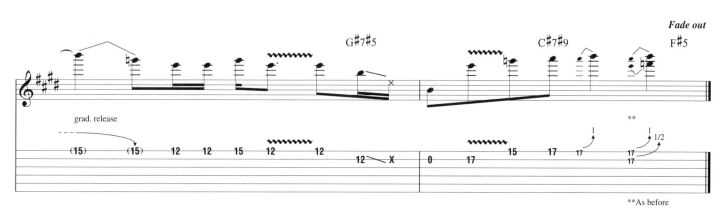

**As before

37

from *Tore Down House*
Dolemite
Written by Scott Henderson

Tune down 1/2 step:
(low to high) E♭-A♭-D♭-G♭-B♭-E♭

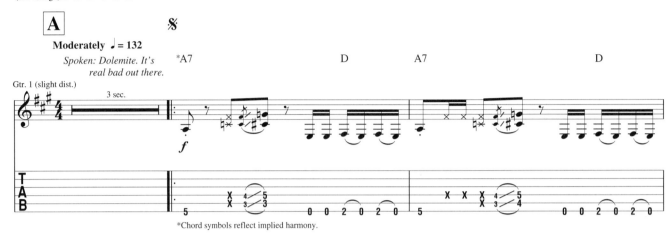

*Chord symbols reflect implied harmony.

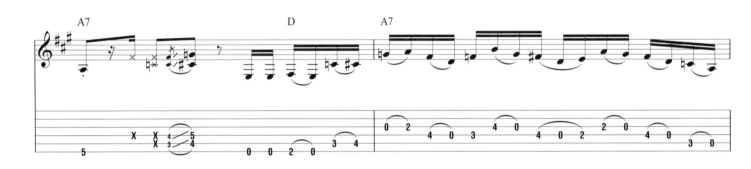

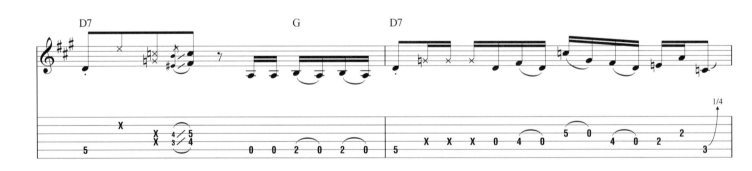

5th time, To Coda 2

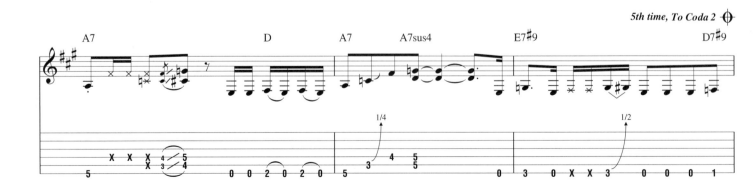

40

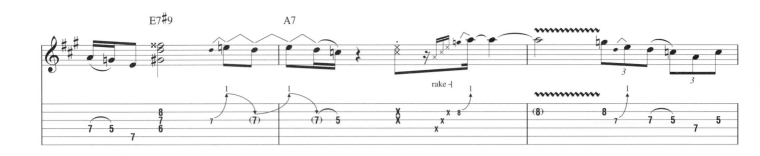

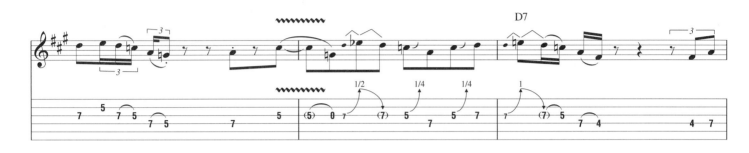

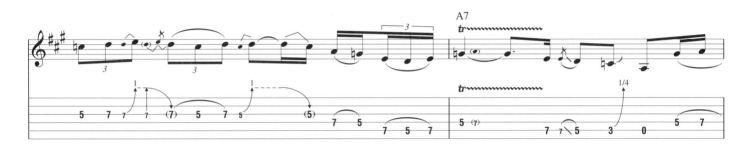

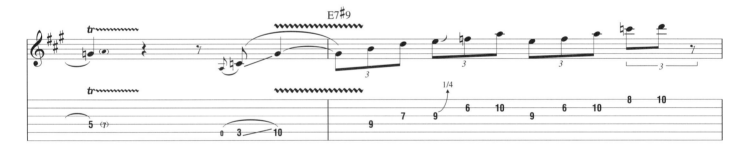

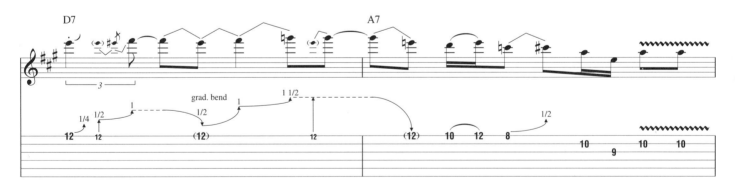

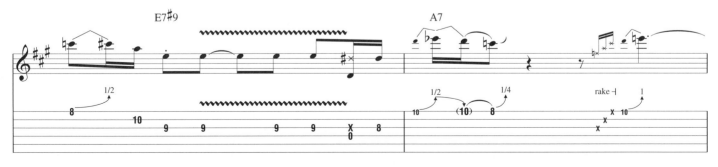

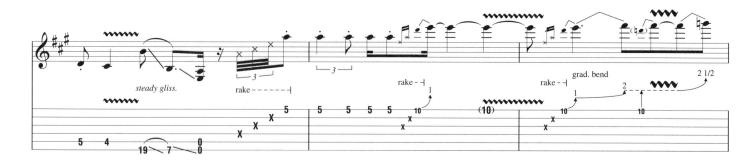

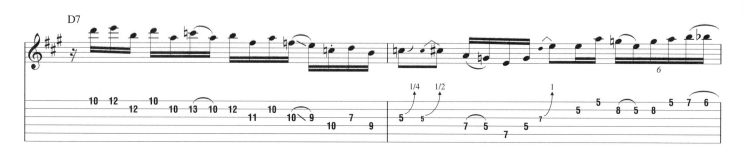

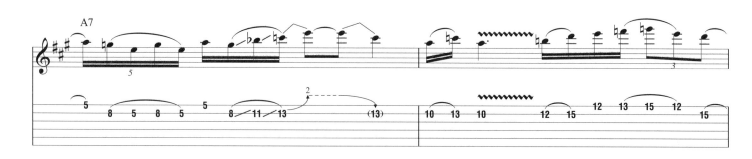

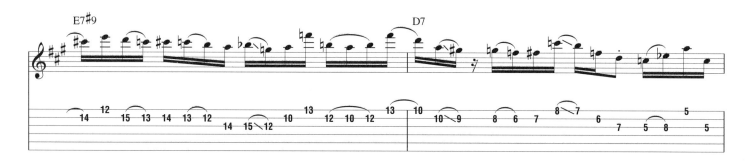

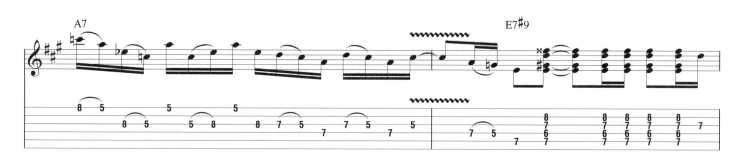

44

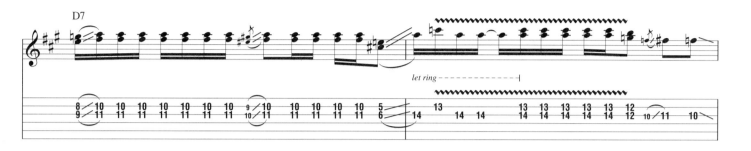

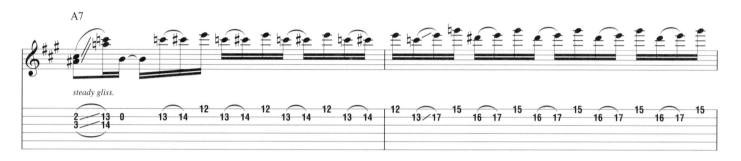

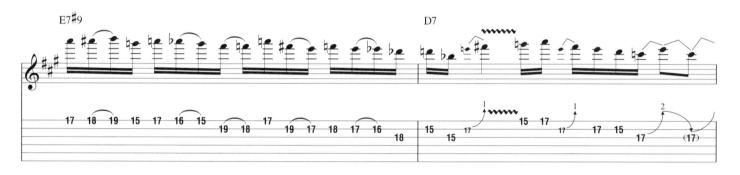

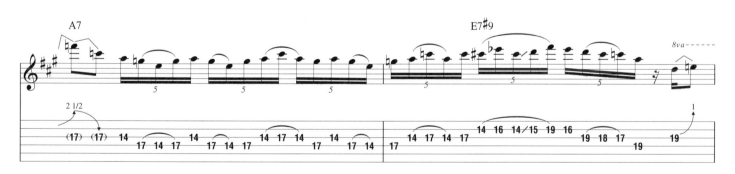

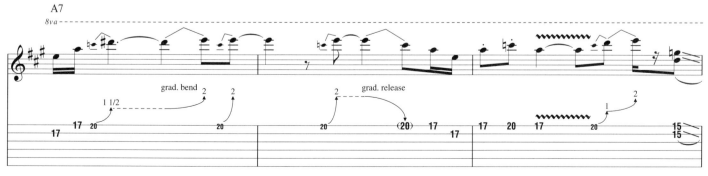

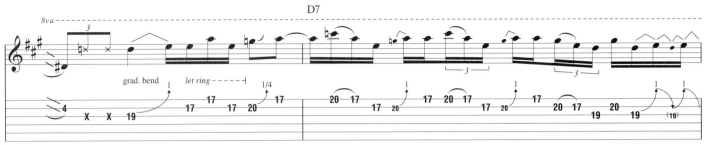

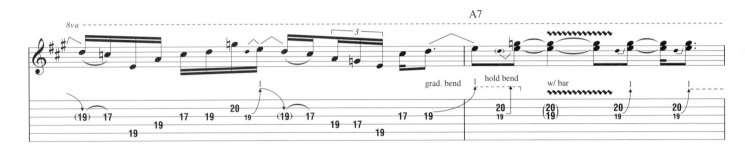

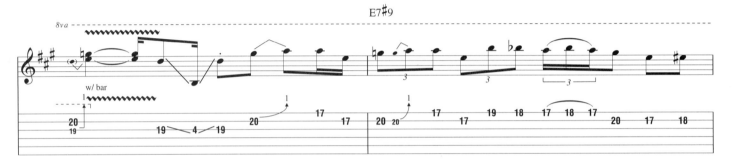

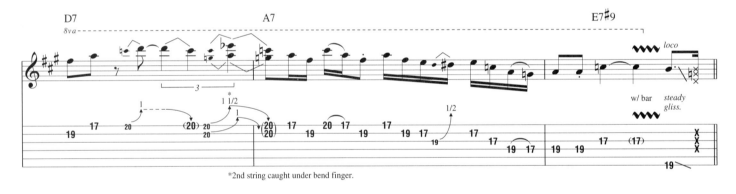

*2nd string caught under bend finger.

E

D.S. al Coda 2
(take repeat)

⊕ Coda 2

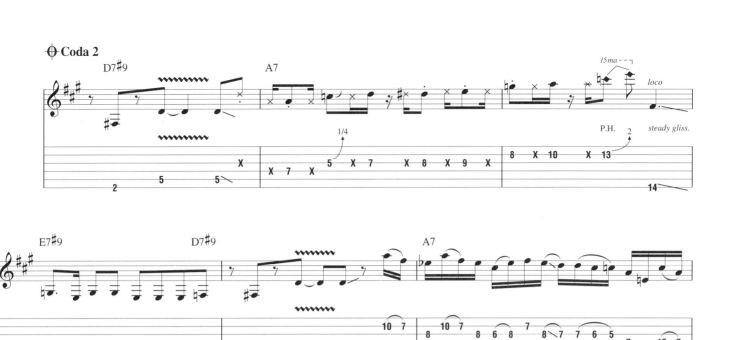

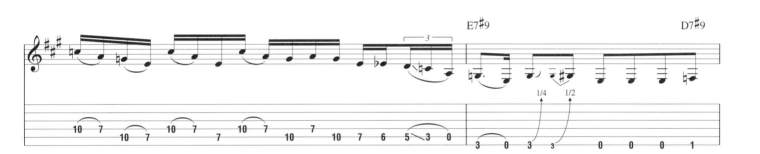

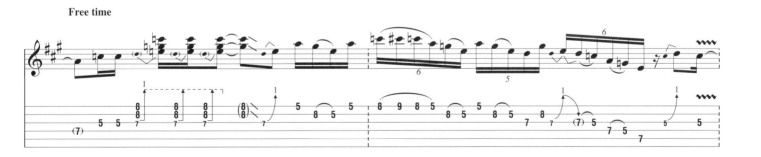

Free time

Hole Diggin'

Written by Scott Henderson

Tune down 1/2 step:
(low to high) E♭-A♭-D♭-G♭-B♭-E♭

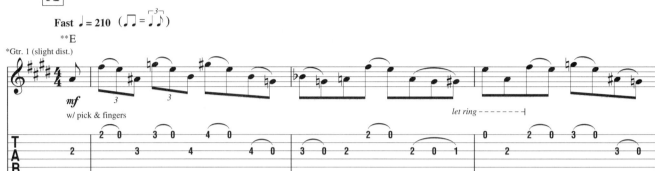

*Use neck pickup.

**Chord symbols reflect implied harmony.

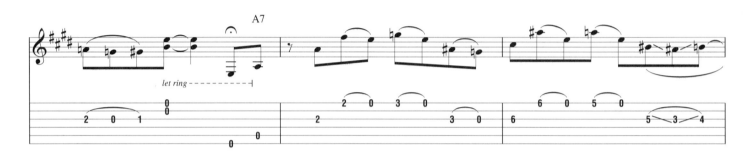

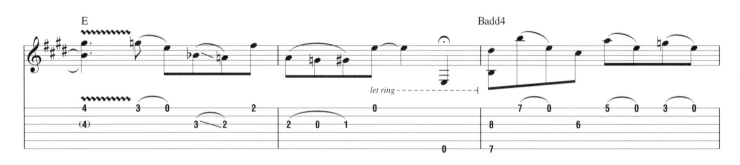

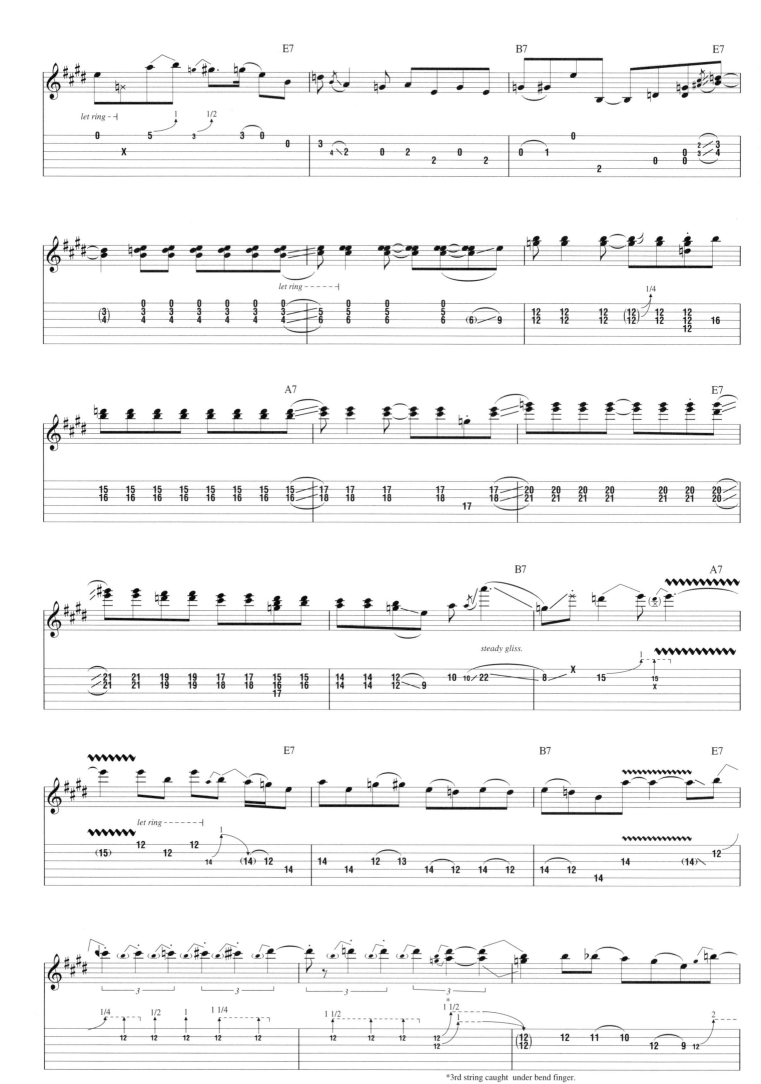

*3rd string caught under bend finger.

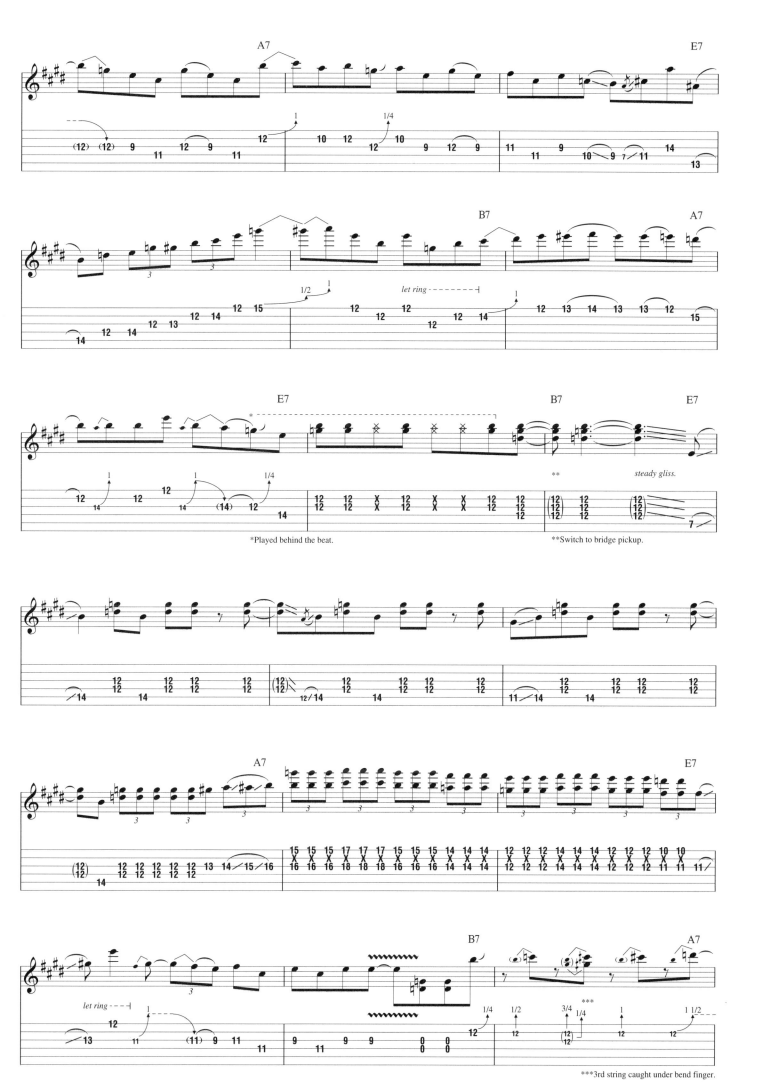

*Played behind the beat.

**Switch to bridge pickup.

***3rd string caught under bend finger.

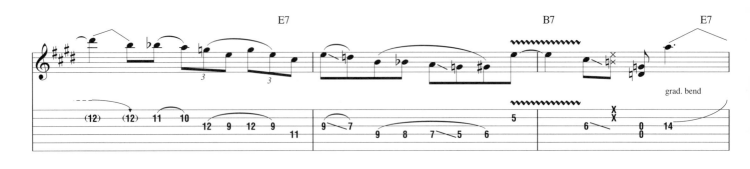

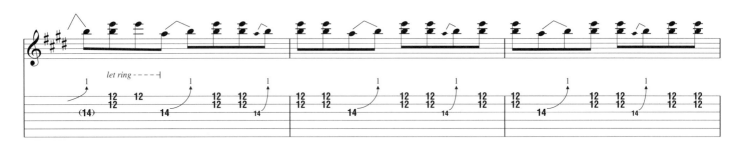

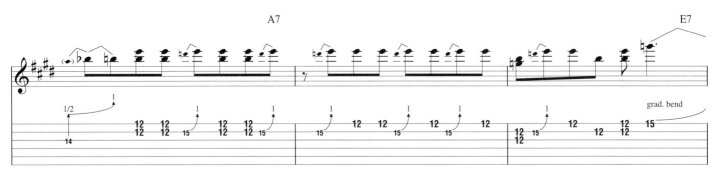

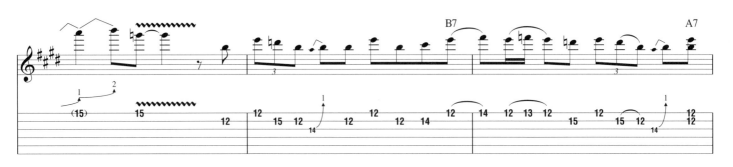

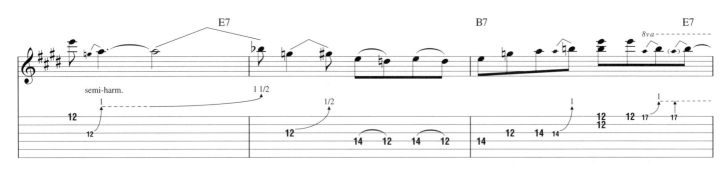

*Played ahead
of the beat.

*Switch to neck pickup.

*Switch to bridge
pickup.

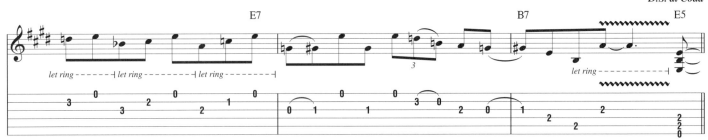

Coda

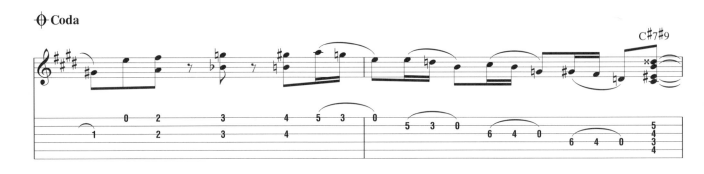

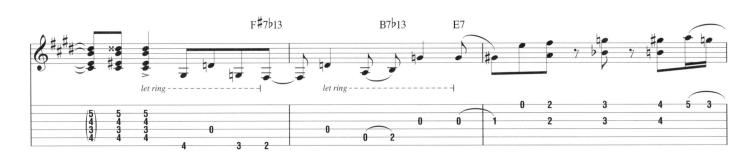

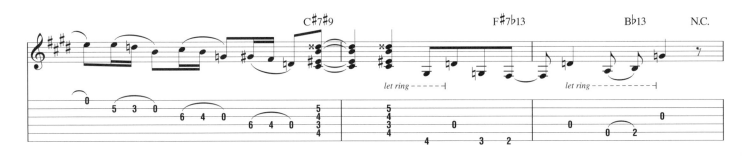

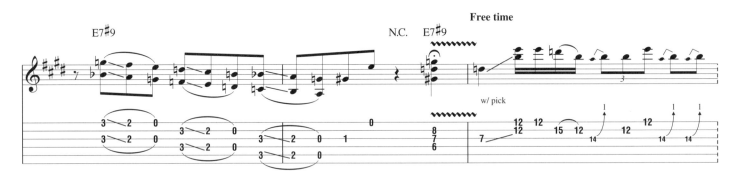

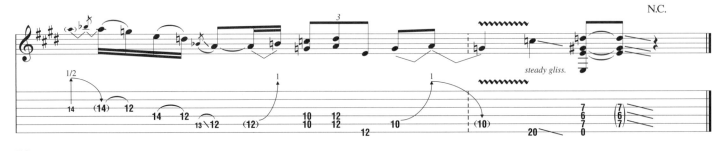

from *Well to the Bone*

Lady P

Written by Scott Henderson

Tune down 1/2 step:
(low to high) Eb-Ab-Db-Gb-Bb-Eb

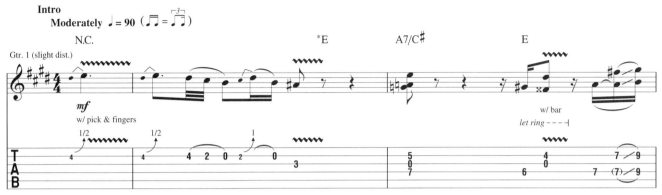

*Chord symbols reflect overall harmony.

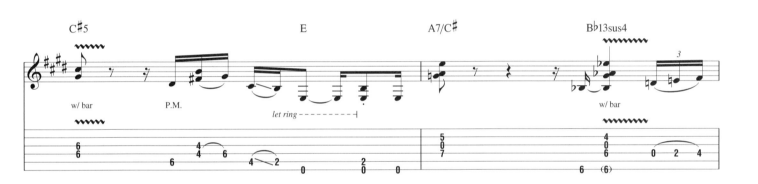

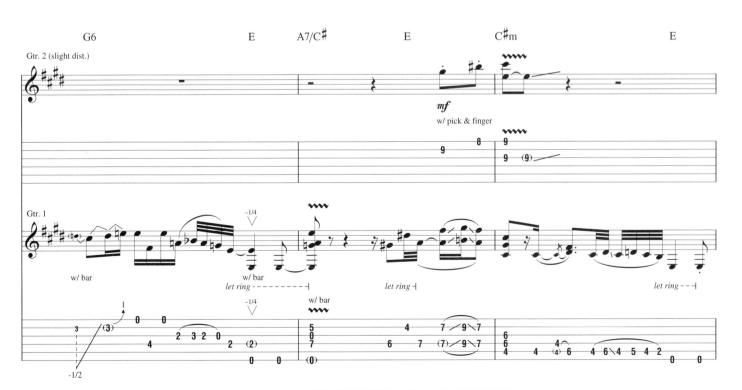

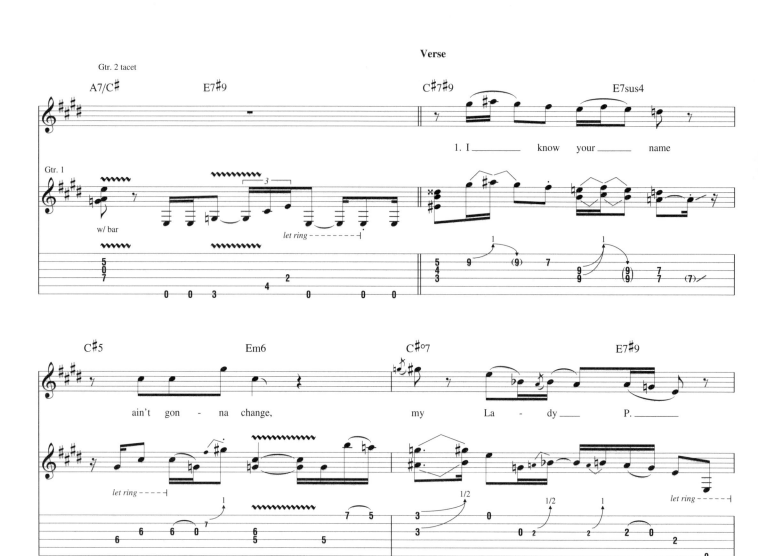

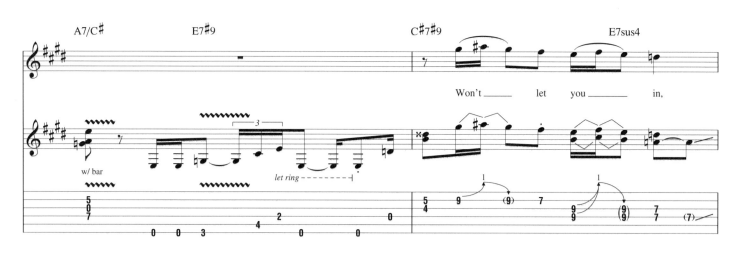

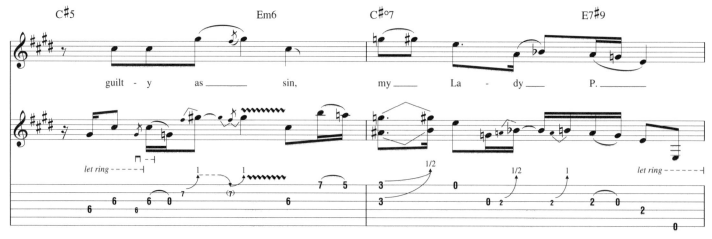

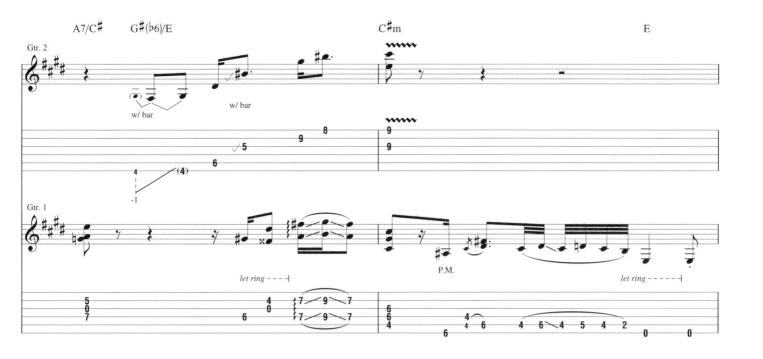
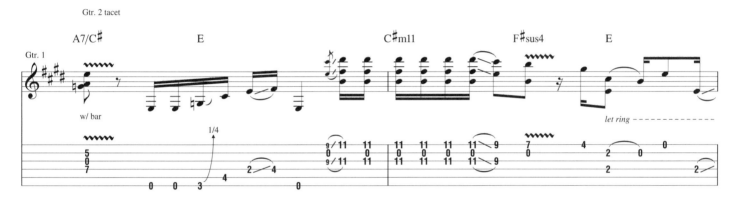
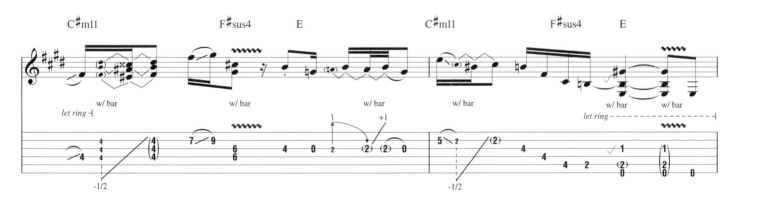
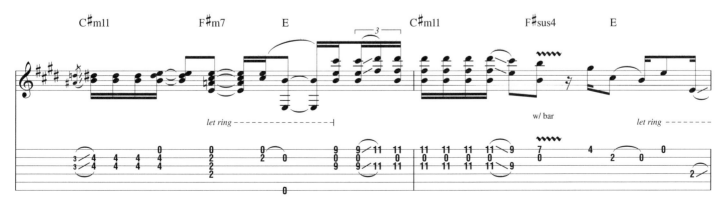

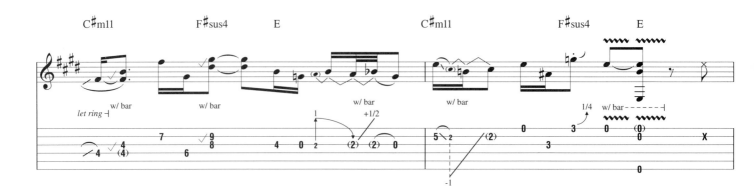

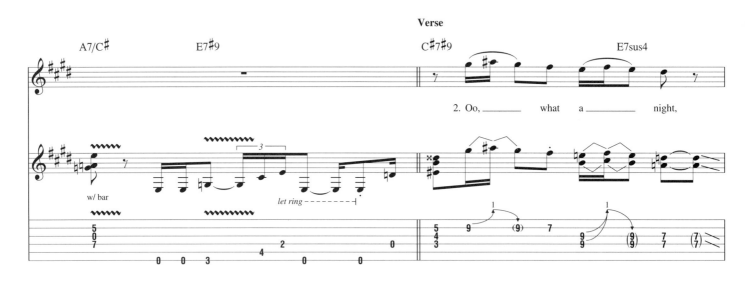

Verse

2. Oo, _____ what a _____ night,

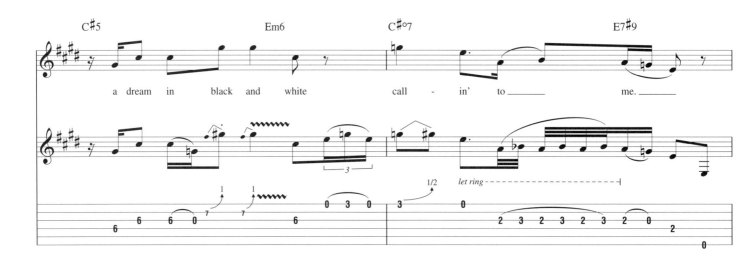

a dream in black and white call - in' to _____ me. _____

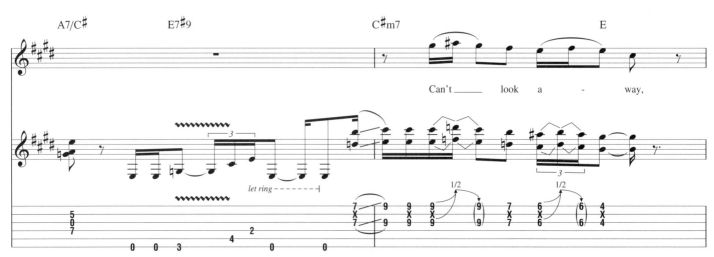

Can't _____ look a - way,

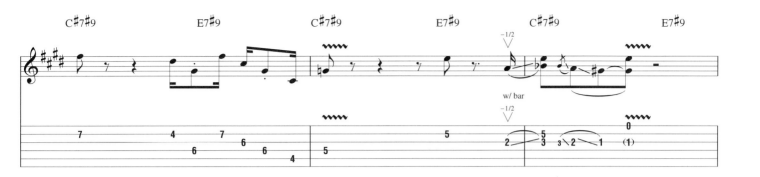

Pitch: A   D   E   A   D   G   D

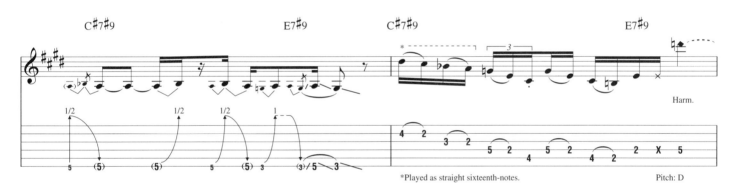

*Played as straight sixteenth-notes.

Pitch: D

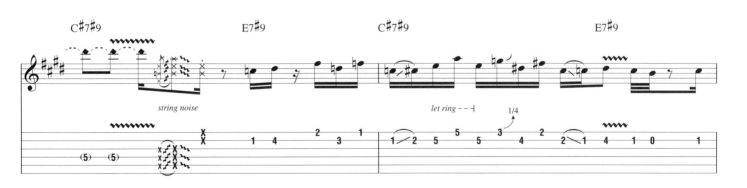

**Played behind the beat.

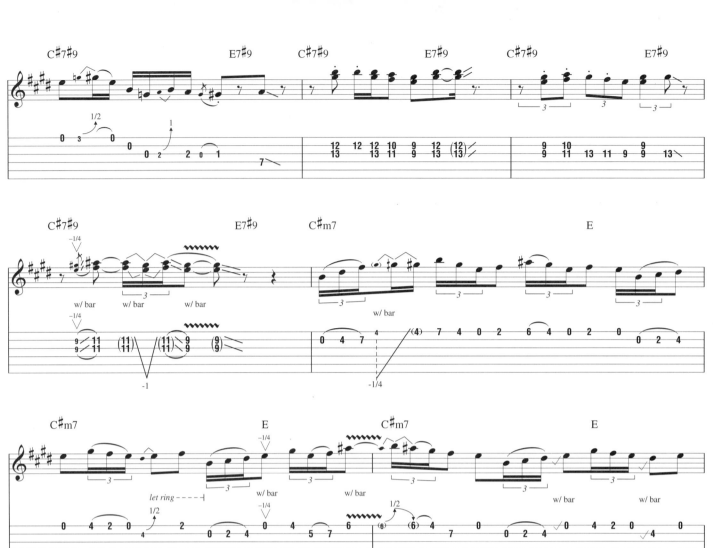

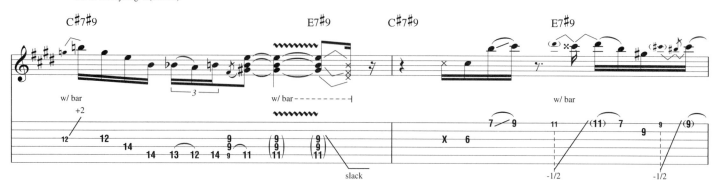

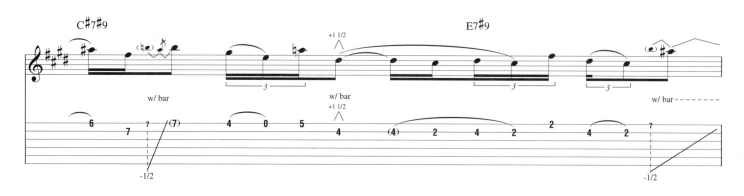

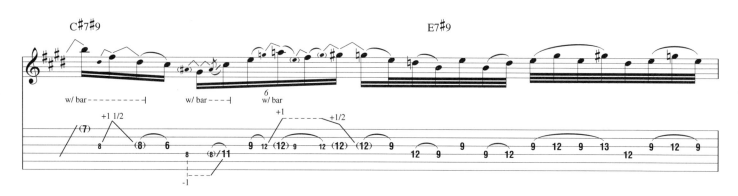

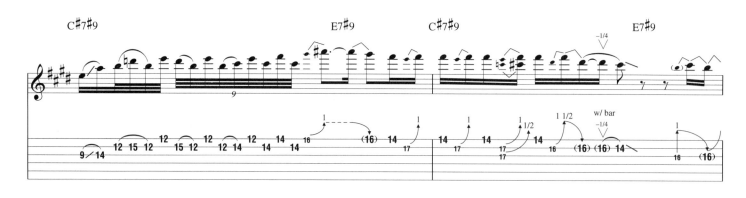

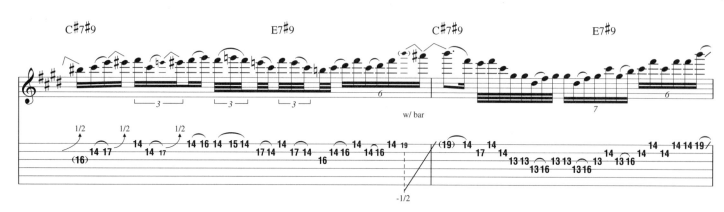

Interlude

Gtr. 2 tacet

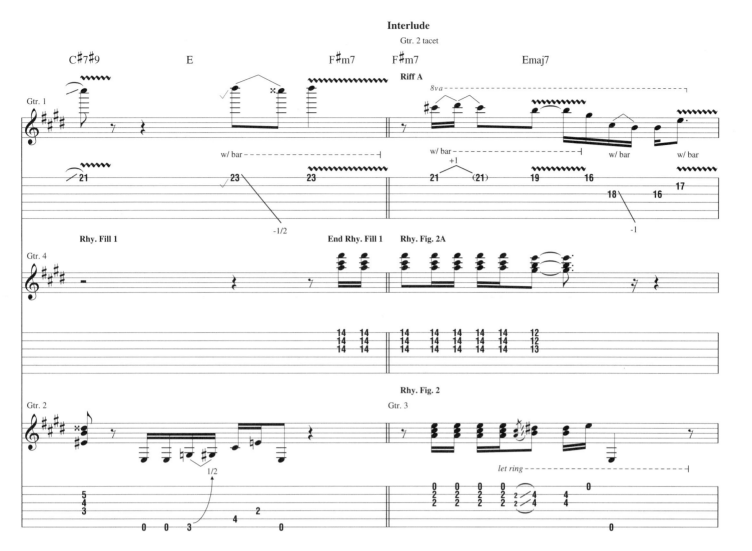

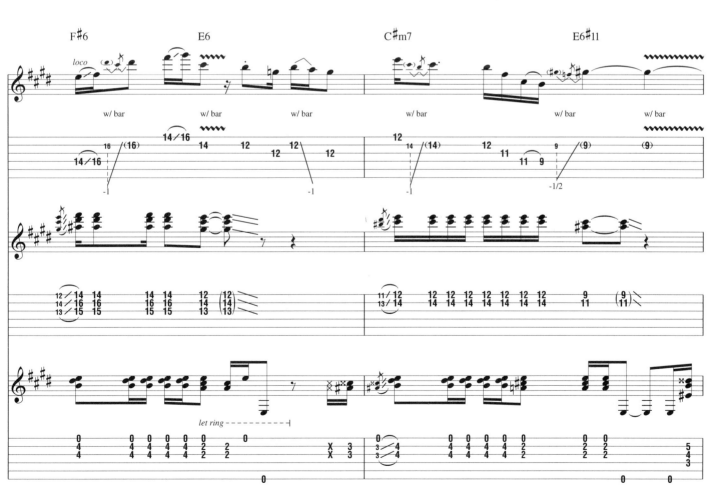

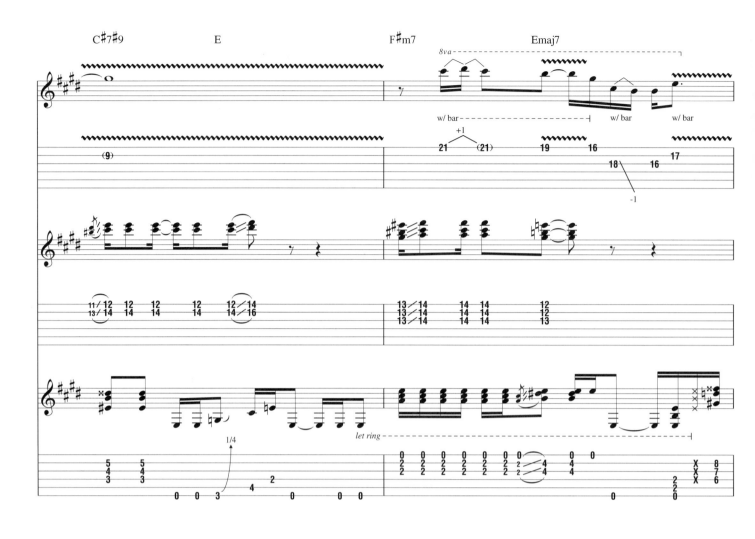

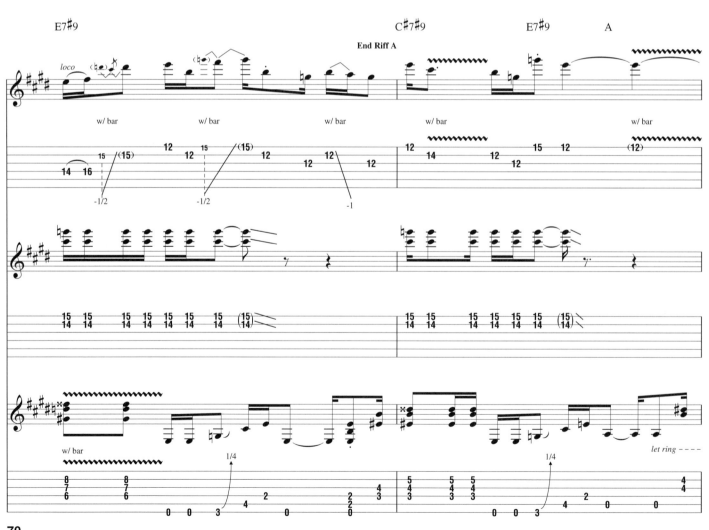

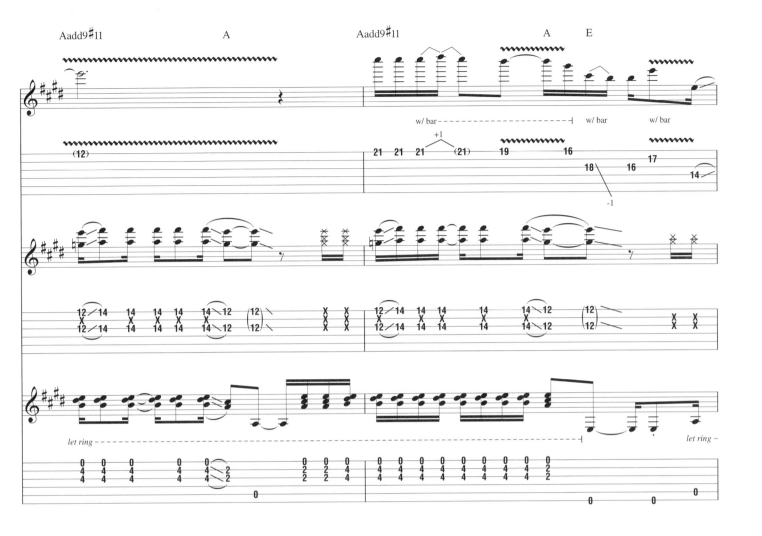

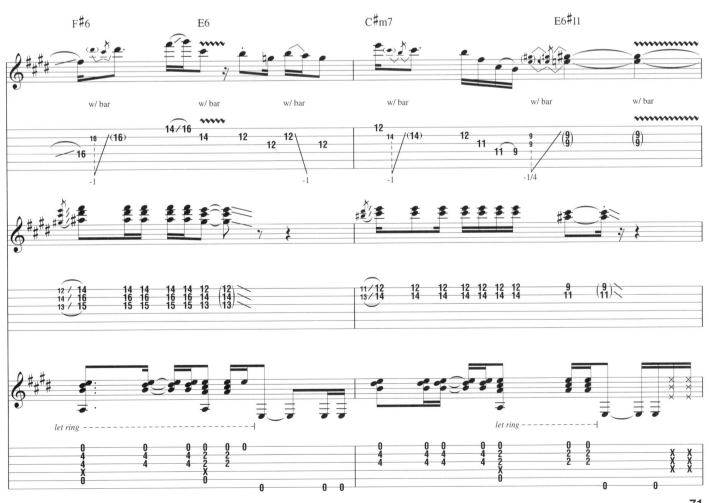

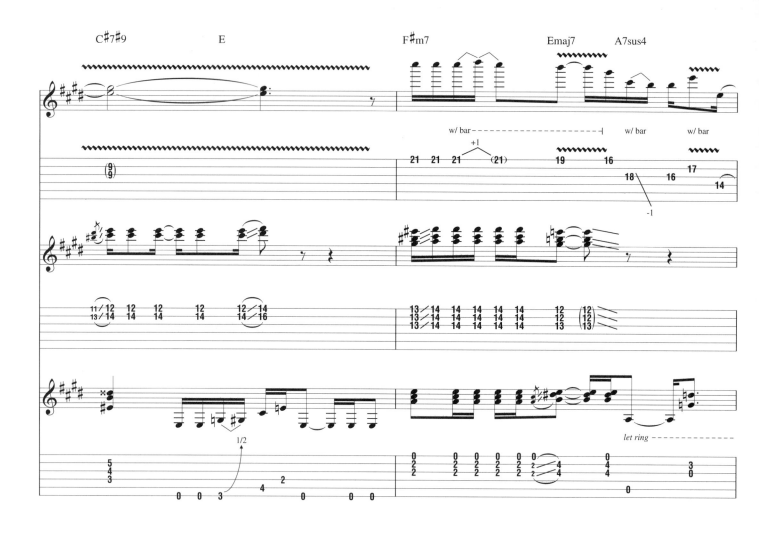

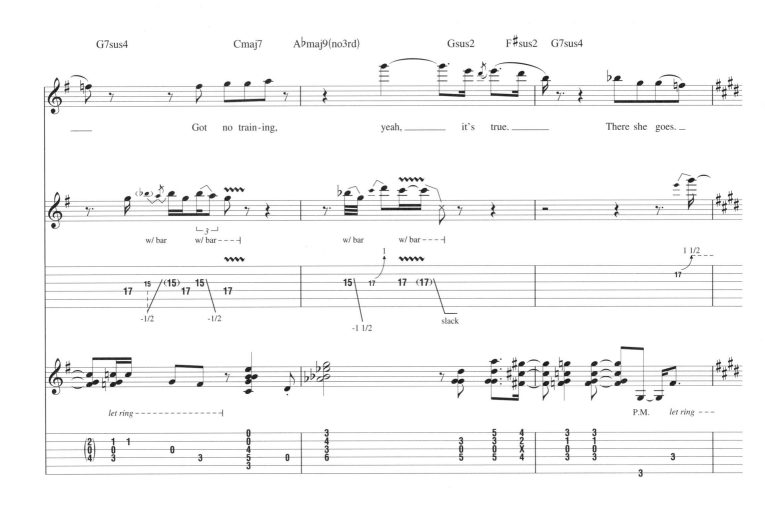

Got no train-ing,   yeah, _____ it's true. _____ There she goes. _

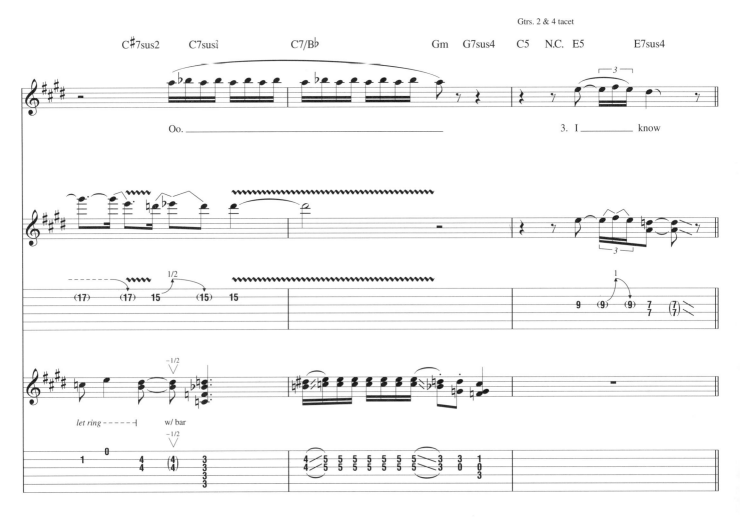

Oo. _____ 3. I _____ know

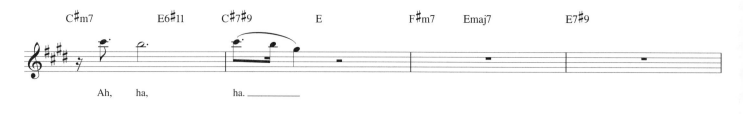

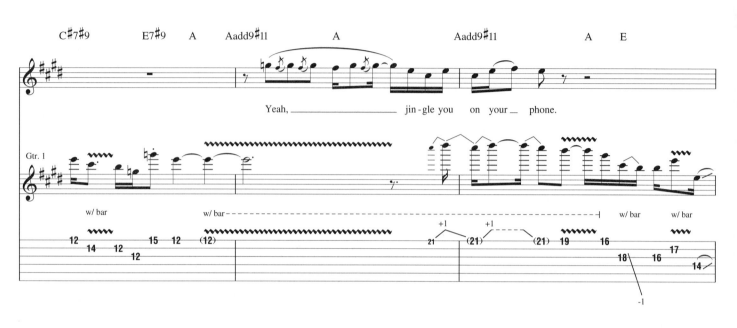

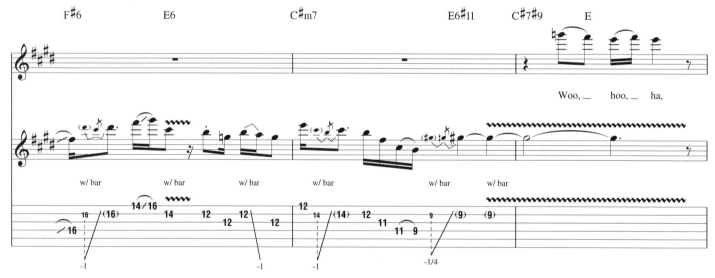

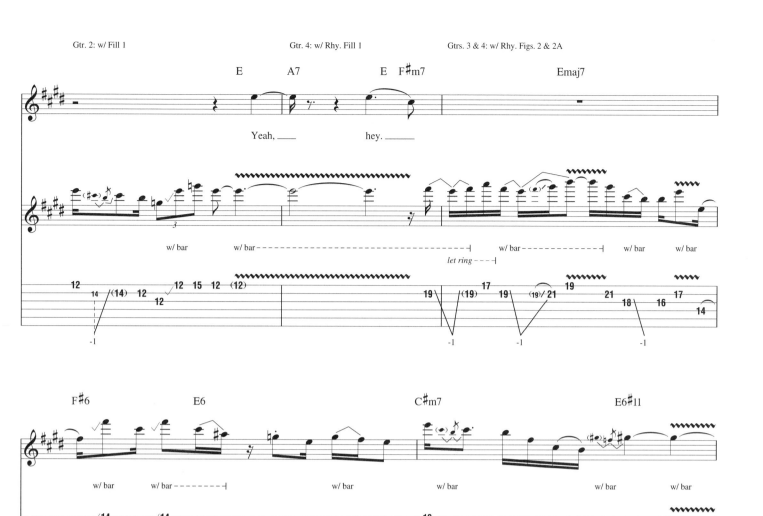

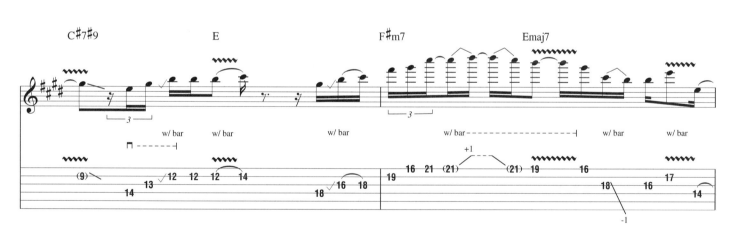

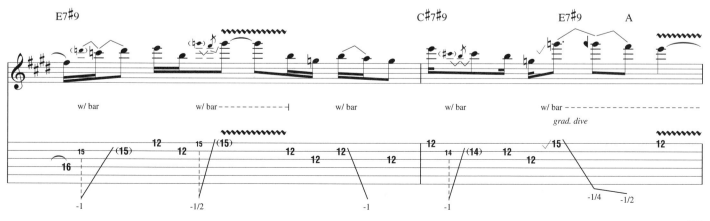

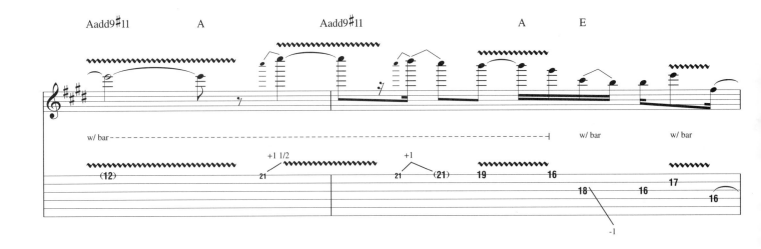

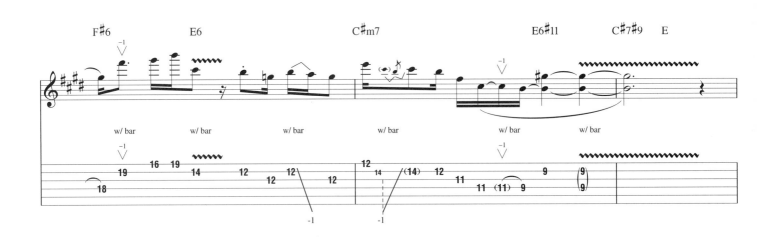

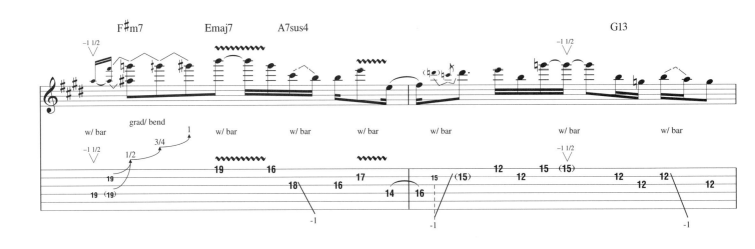

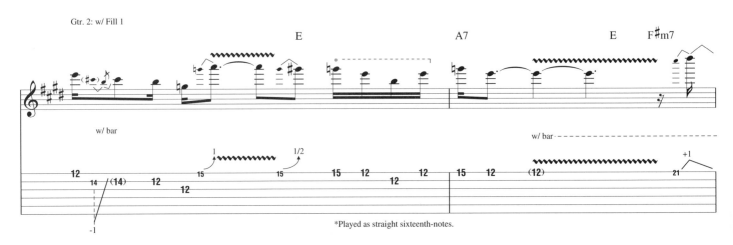

*Played as straight sixteenth-notes.

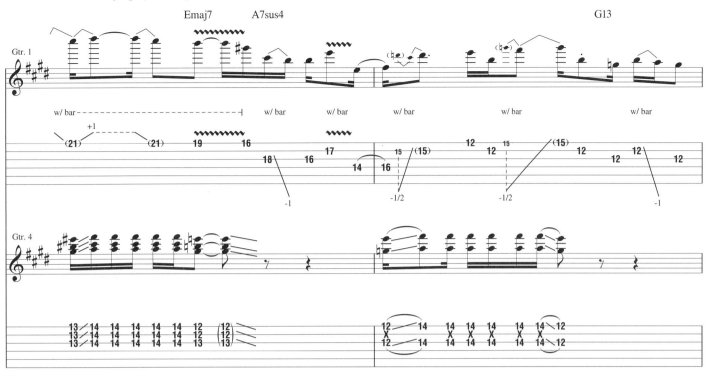

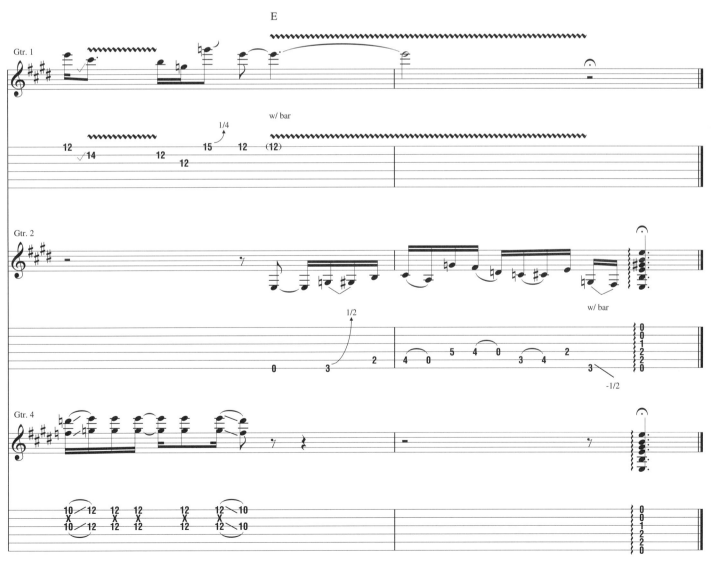

from *Tore Down House*
Meter Maid
Written by Scott Henderson

Tune down 1/2 step:
(low to high) E♭-A♭-D♭-G♭-B♭-E♭

Verse
Moderately ♩ = 105

1. I'm com-ing to ru-in your day. ___ I'm a bad old ug-ly me-ter maid. ___

Gtr. 1 (slight dist.)

mf

*Chord symbols reflect basic harmony.

Just go and ask ___ for my ___ man, Je-rome, _____ he says I'm

mean work-ing but I'm mean-er at home. ___

Interlude

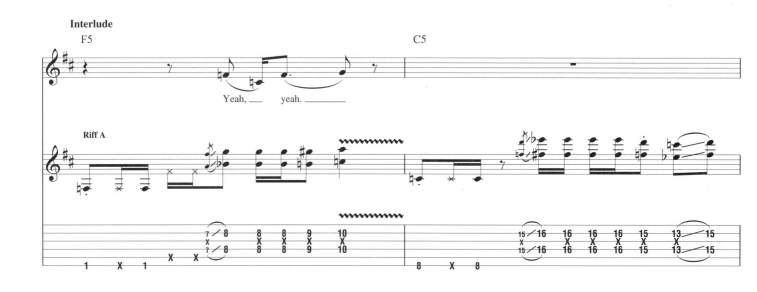

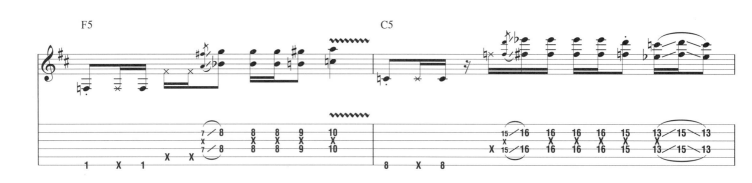

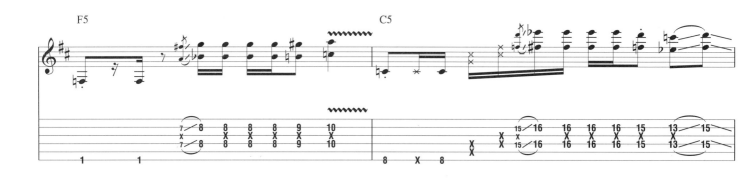

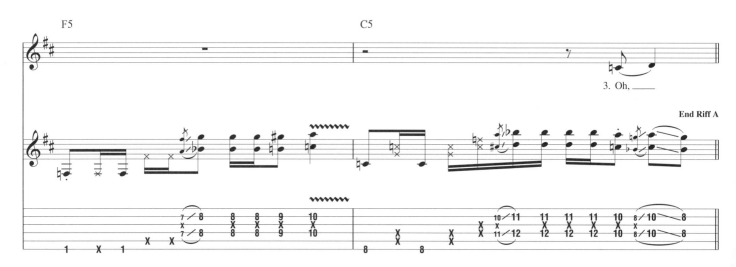

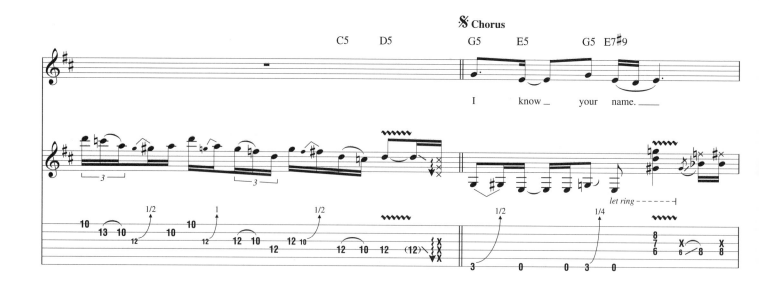

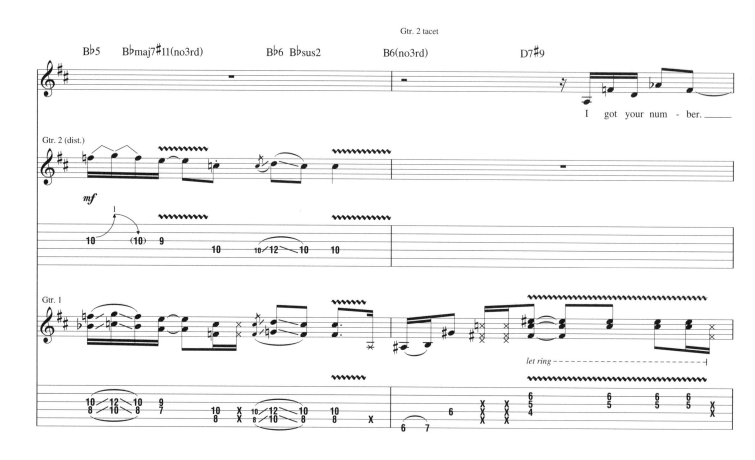

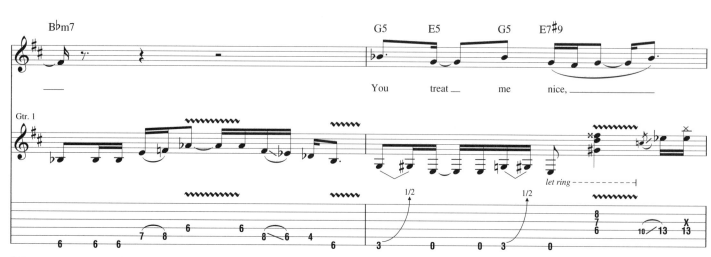

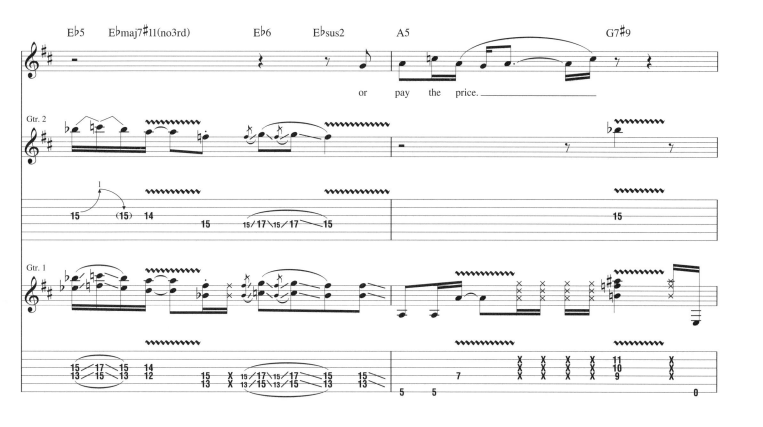

To Coda ⊕

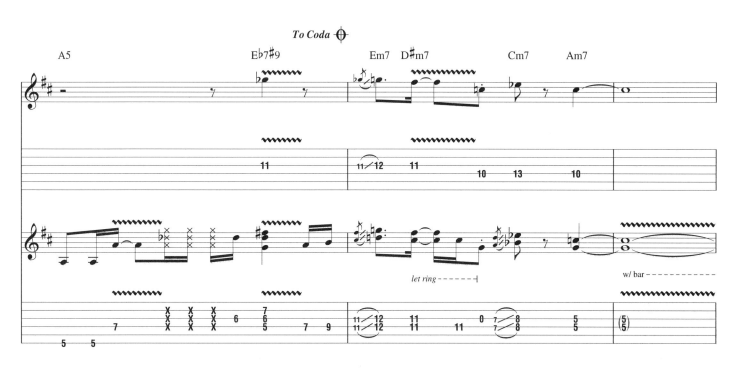

Guitar Solo

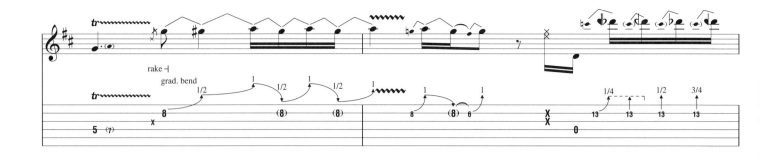

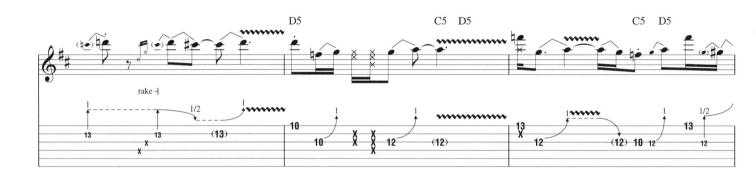

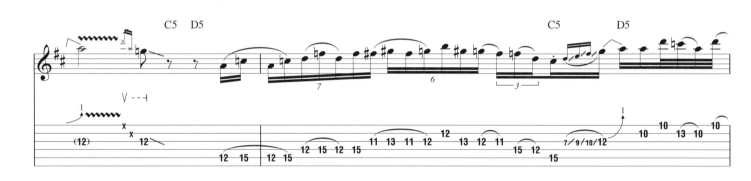

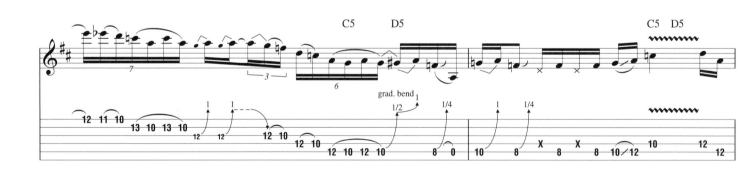

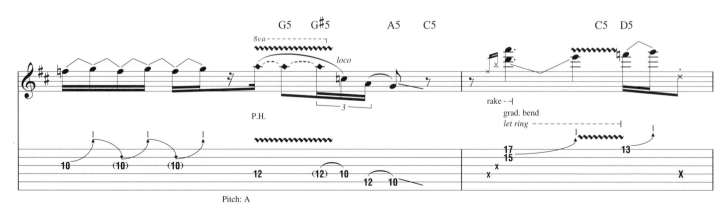

Pitch: A

*2nd string caught under bend finger.

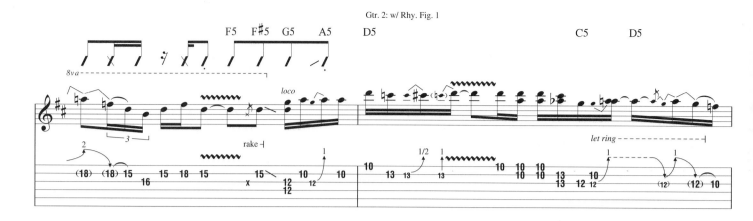

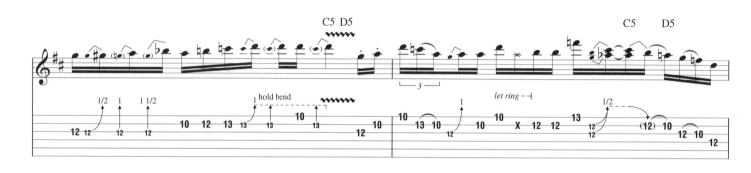

Interlude

Gtr. 1: w/ Riff A
Gtr. 2 tacet

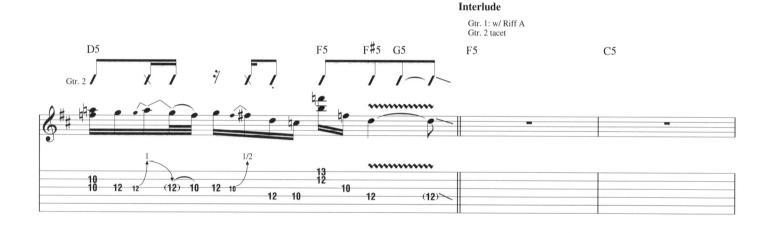

Verse

Gtr. 2 tacet

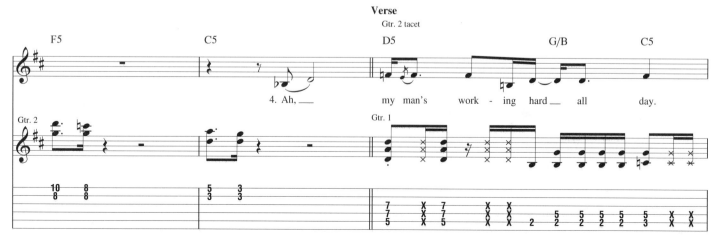

4. Ah, ____ my man's work-ing hard ___ all day.

*2nd string caught under bend finger.   **As before

D.S. al Coda

⊕ Coda

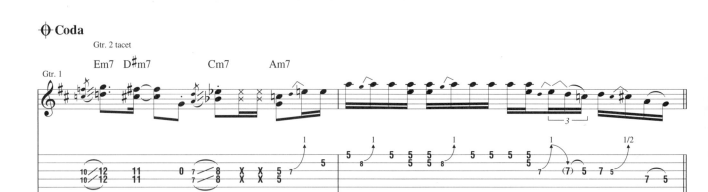

Verse

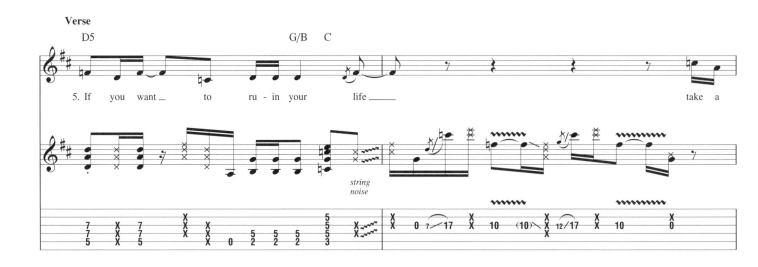

5. If you want ___ to ru-in your life _____ take a

bad, old me-ter maid for your wife _____ Uh, just

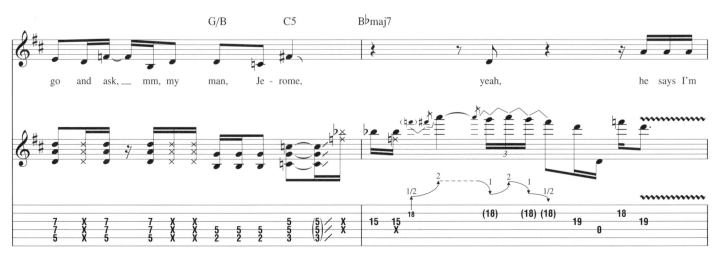

go and ask, ___ mm, my man, Je-rome, yeah, he says I'm

from *Dog Party*

Same As You

Written by Scott Henderson

Gtrs. 1 & 3: Tune down 1/2 step:
(low to high) Eb-Ab-Db-Gb-Bb-Eb

Gtr. 2: Tuning:
(low to high) Eb-Ab-Db-Gb-Bb-Db

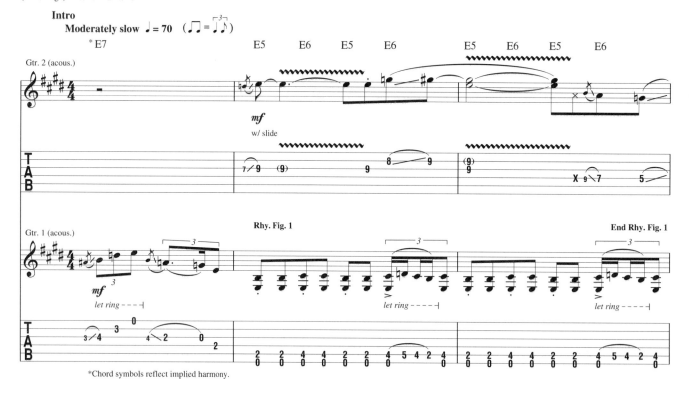

*Chord symbols reflect implied harmony.

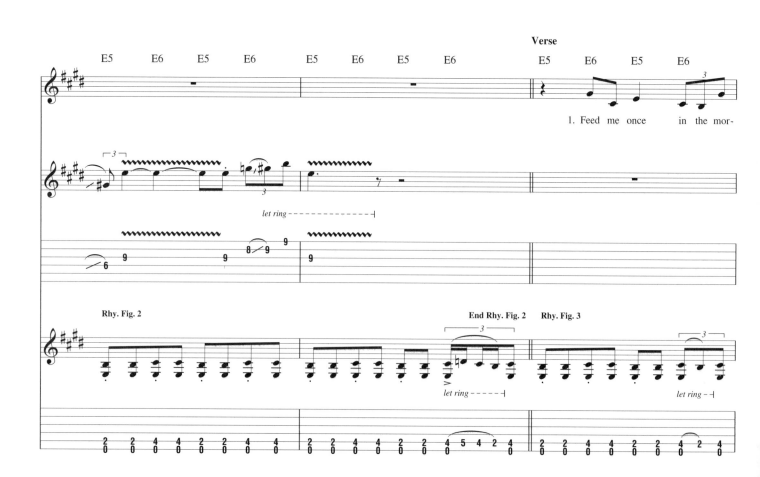

Chorus

Gtr. 2 tacet

*Gtr. 3 (elec.) w/ clean tone, played *mf*.
Composite arrangement

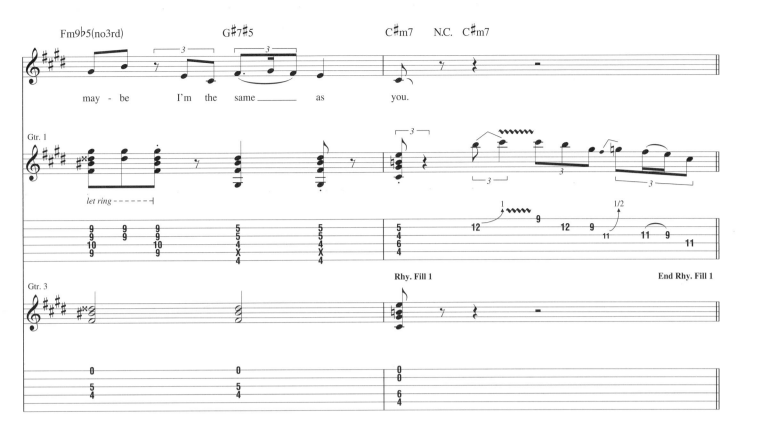

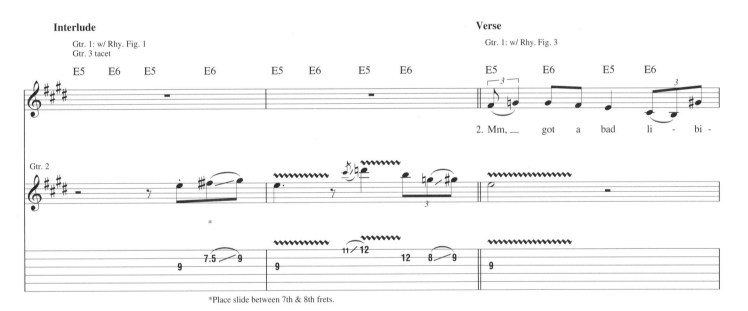

*Place slide between 7th & 8th frets.

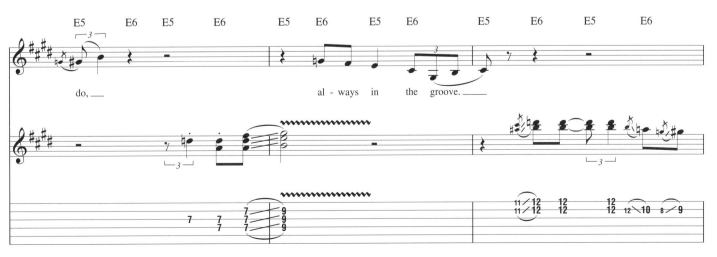

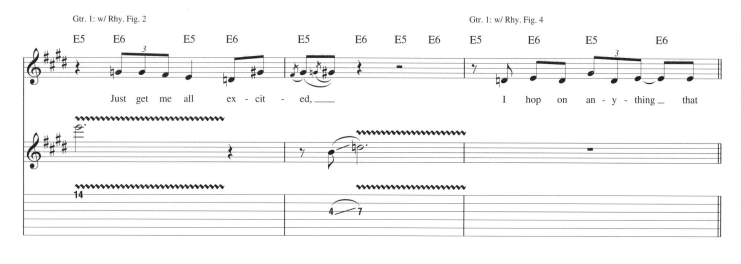

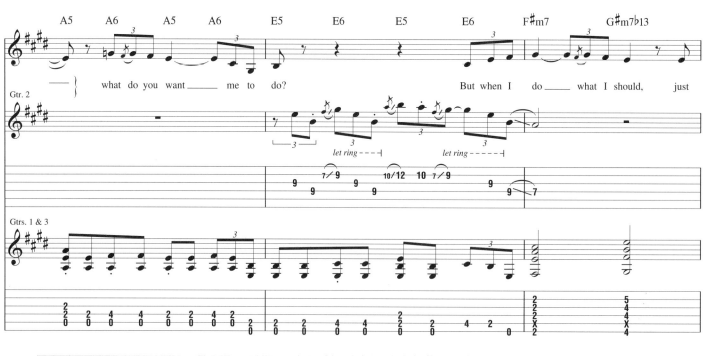

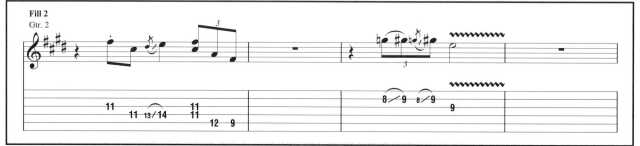

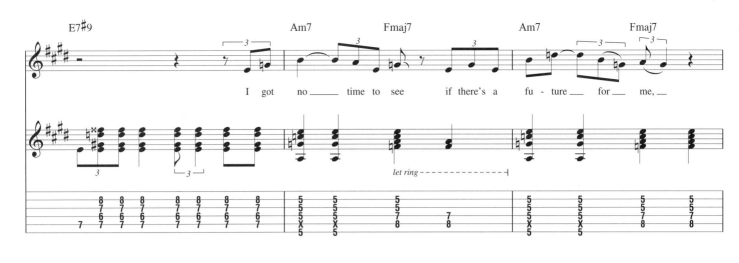

I got no _____ time to see if there's a fu-ture _____ for _____ me, _____

let ring ---------------

Verse
Gtr. 1: w/ Rhy. Fig. 2 (2 times)
Gtr. 3 tacet

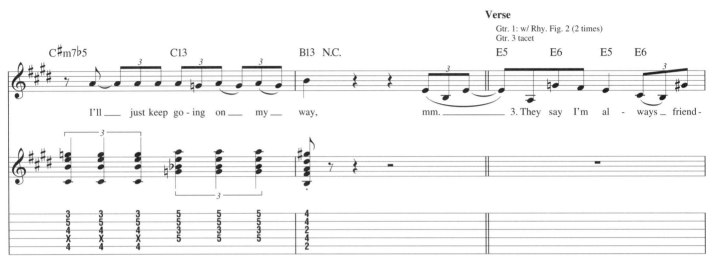

I'll _____ just keep go-ing on _____ my _____ way, mm. _____ 3. They say I'm al-ways _____ friend-

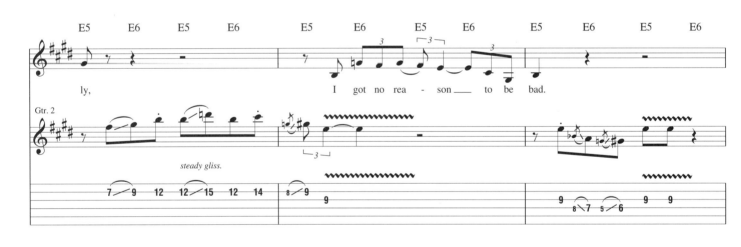

ly, I got no rea-son _____ to be bad.

Gtr. 2

steady gliss.

Gtr. 1: w/ Rhy. Fig. 3 (last 2 meas.)

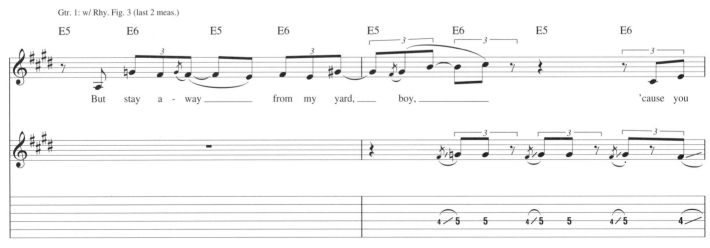

But stay a-way _____ from my yard, _____ boy, _____ 'cause you

don't wan-na see me when I'm mad. _____ Well, I

⊕ Coda

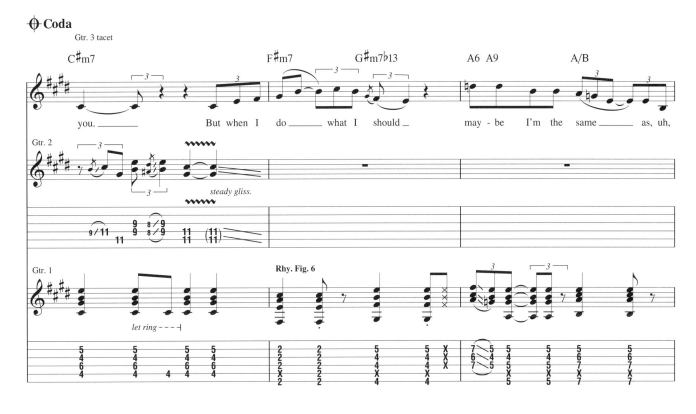

you. _____ But when I do _____ what I should _____ may-be I'm the same _____ as, uh,

you. But when I

*Sung as straight eighth-notes.

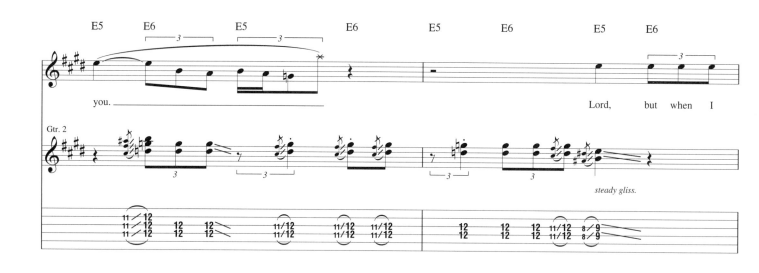

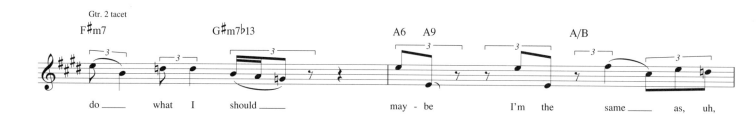

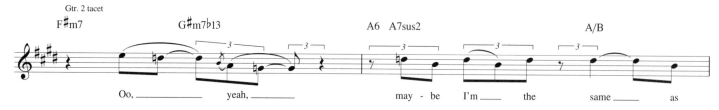

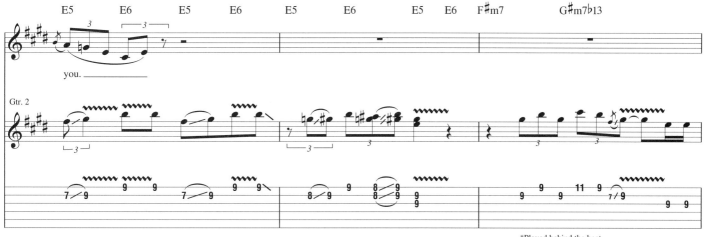

*Played behind the beat.

Begin fade

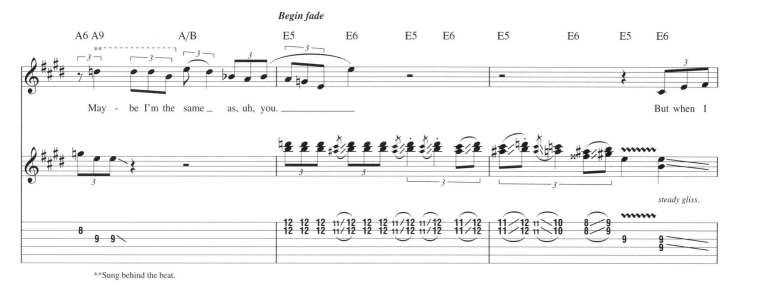

**Sung behind the beat.

Fade out

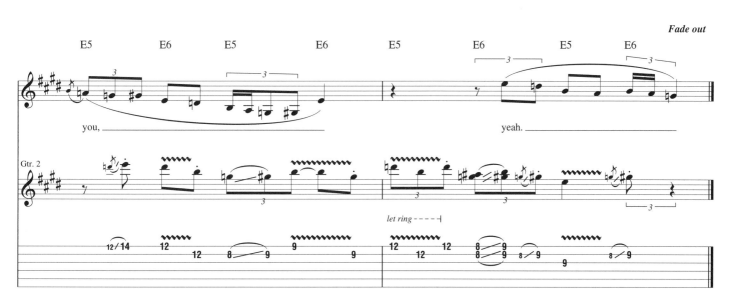

from *Well to the Bone*

That Hurts

Written by Scott Henderson

Tune down 1/2 step:
(low to high) E♭-A♭-D♭-G♭-B♭-E♭

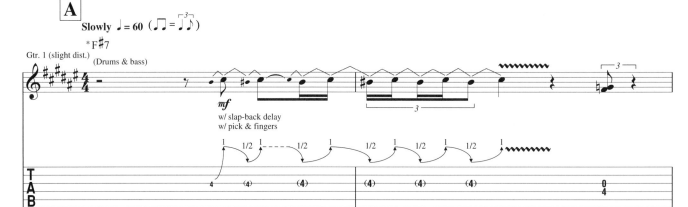

*Chord symbols reflect overall harmony.

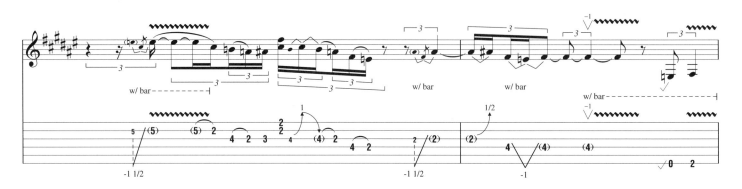

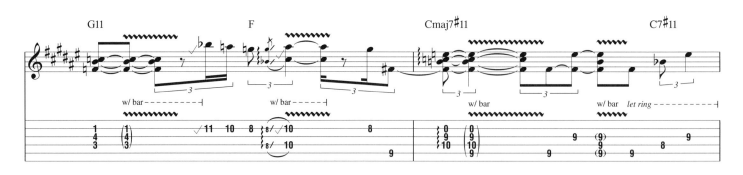

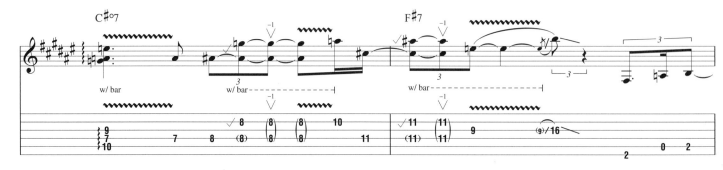

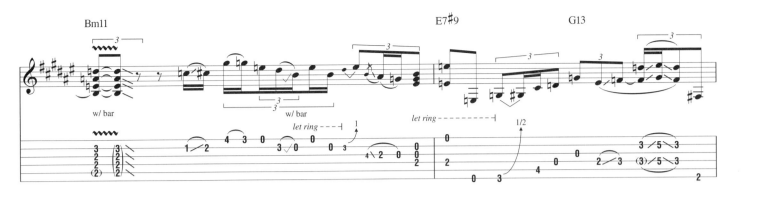

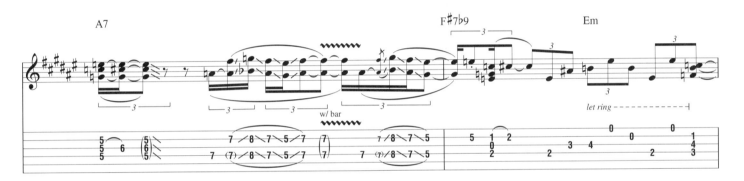

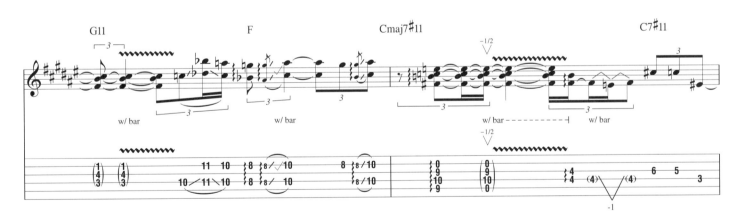

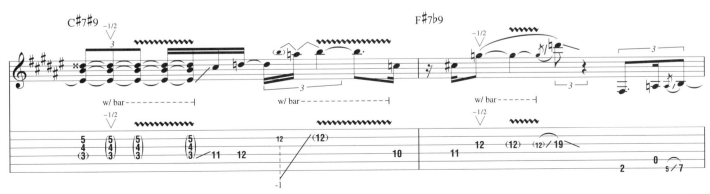

B

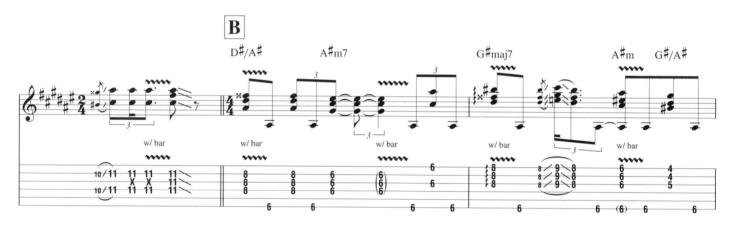

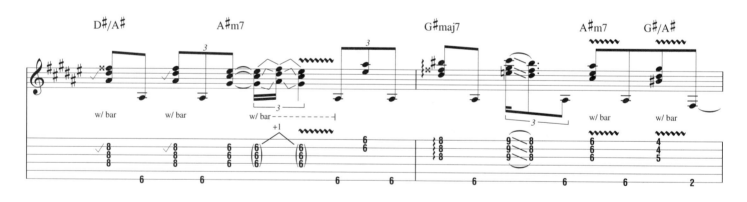

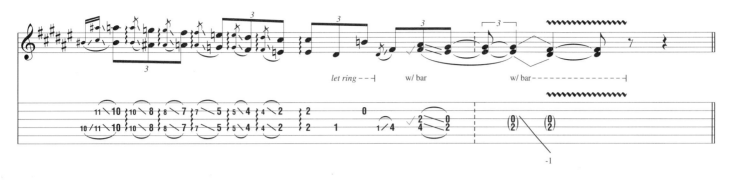

C
A tempo

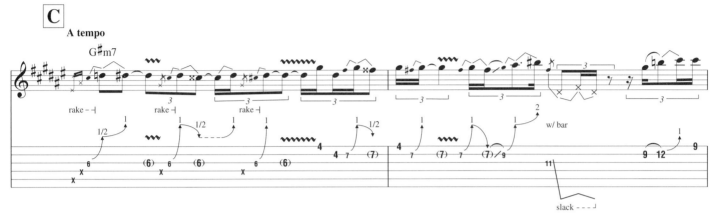

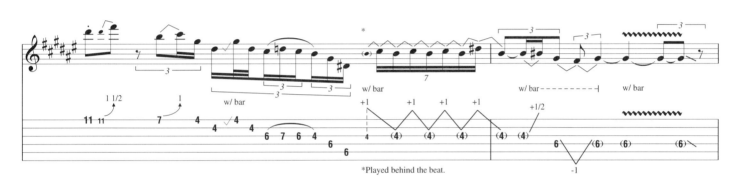

*Played behind the beat.

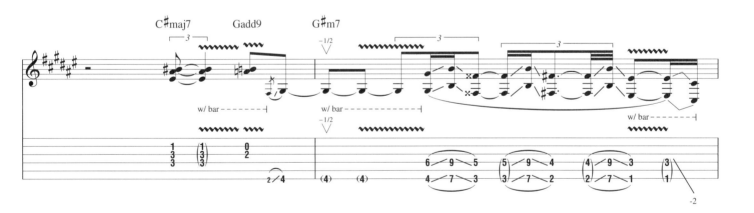

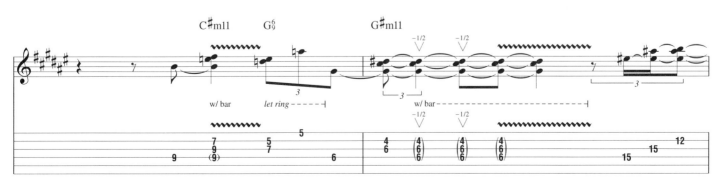

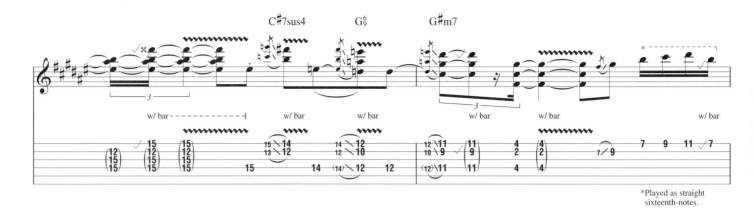

*Played as straight
sixteenth-notes.

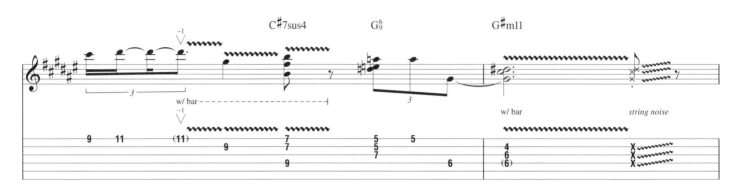

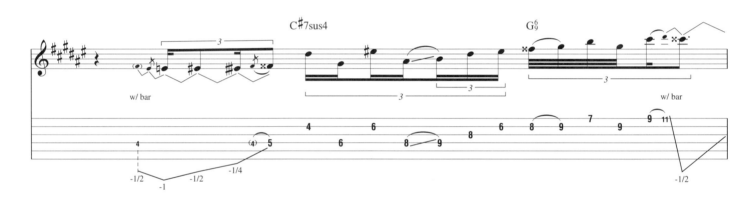

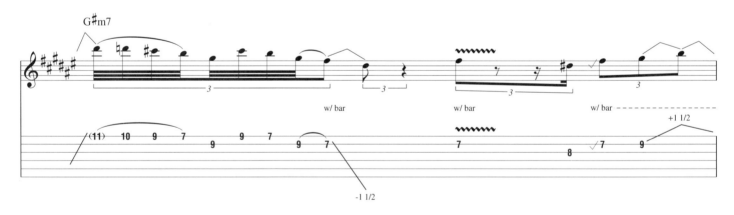

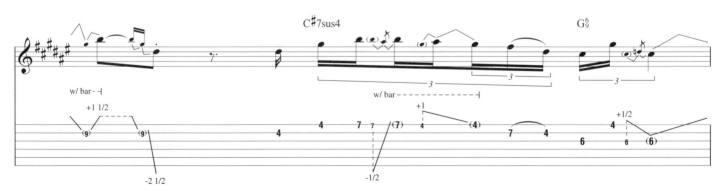

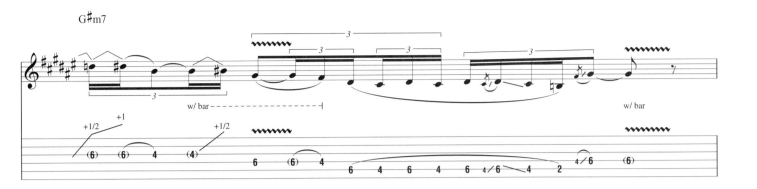

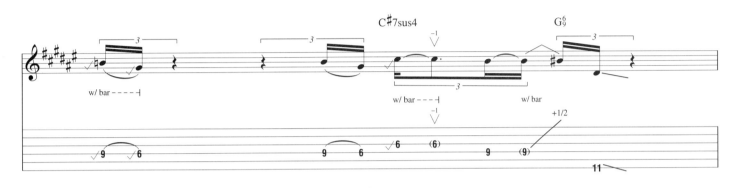

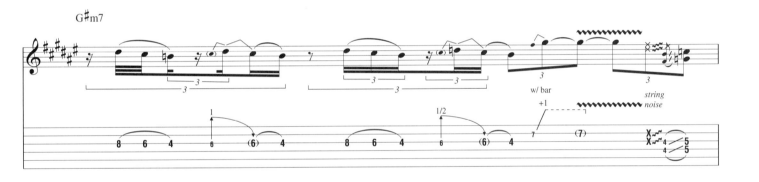

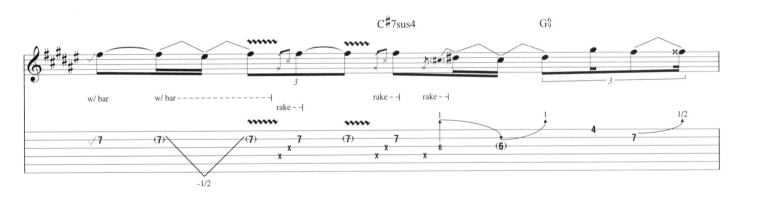

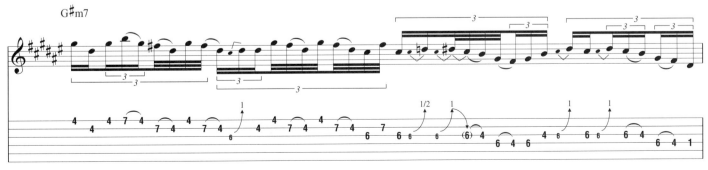

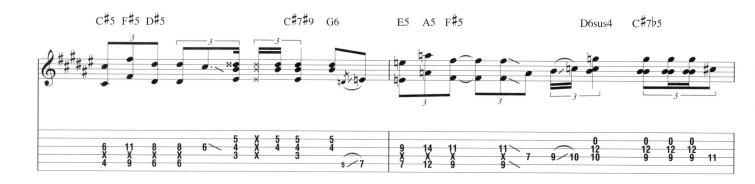

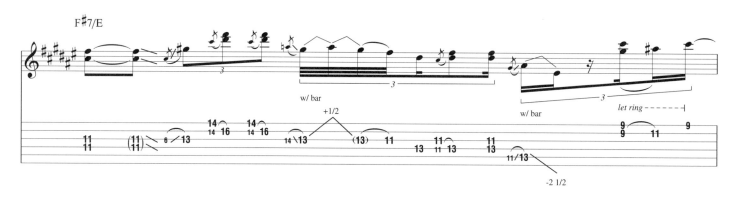

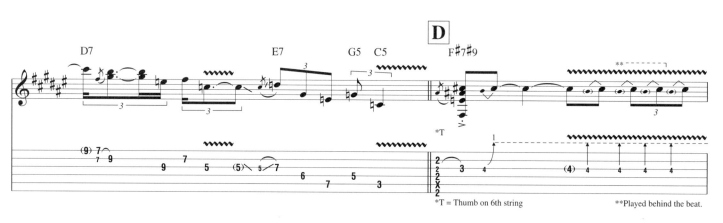

*T = Thumb on 6th string   **Played behind the beat.

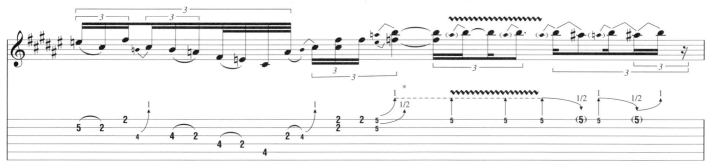

*2nd string caught under bend finger.

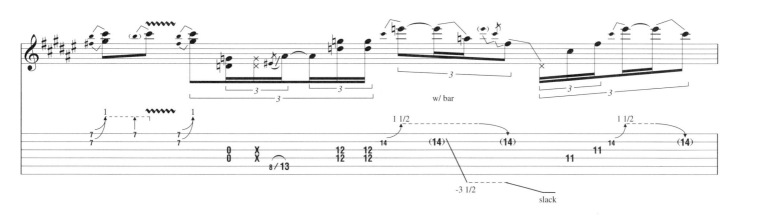

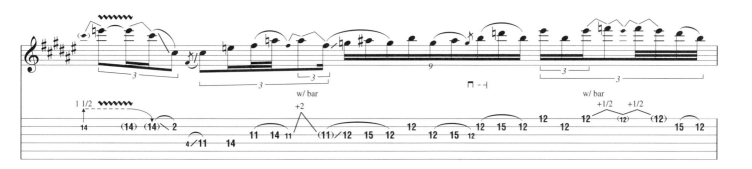

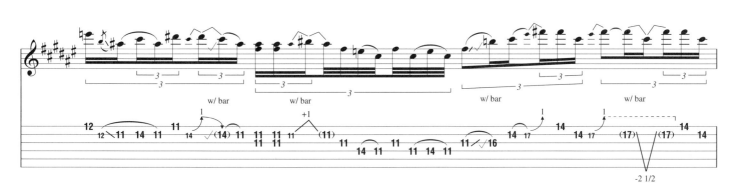

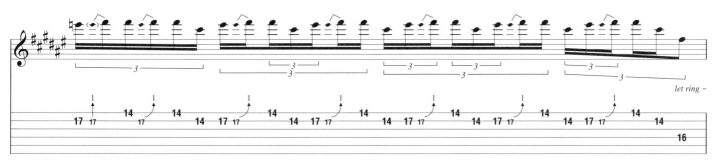

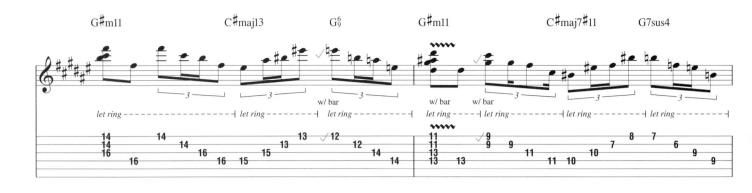

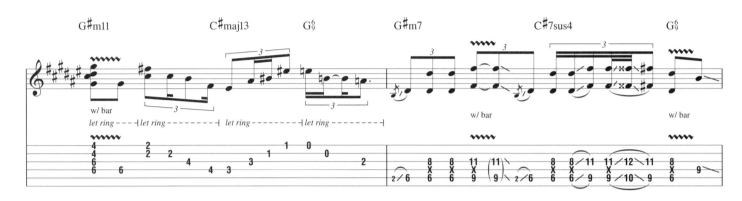

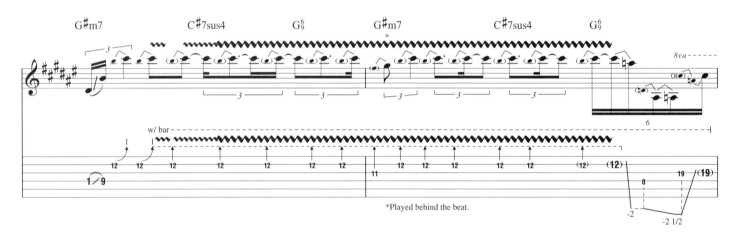

*Played behind the beat.

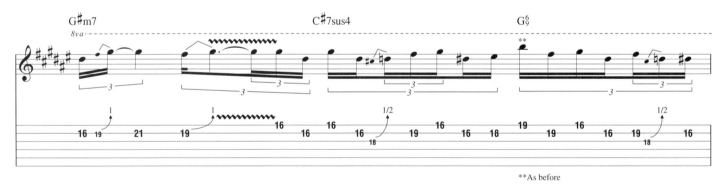

**As before

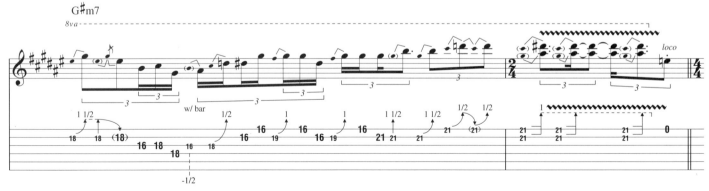

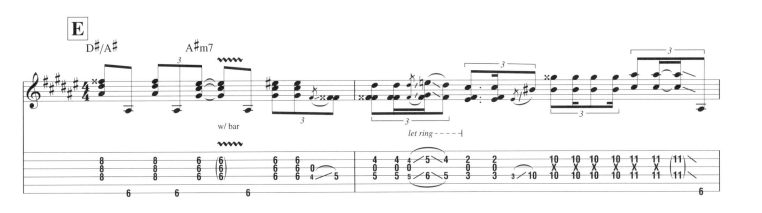

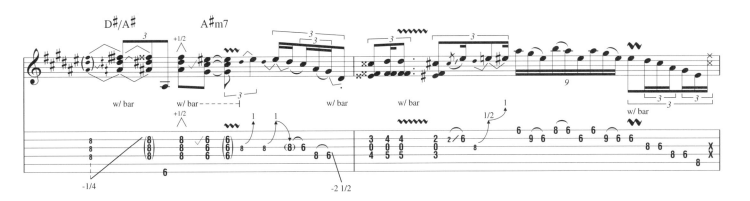

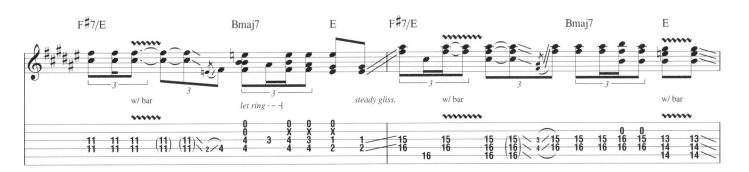

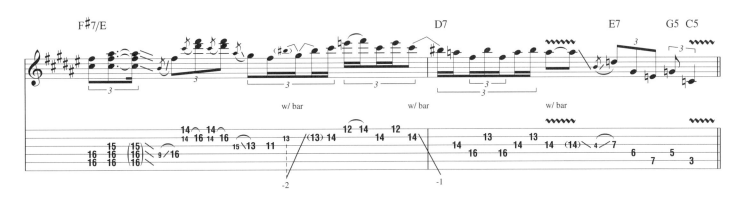

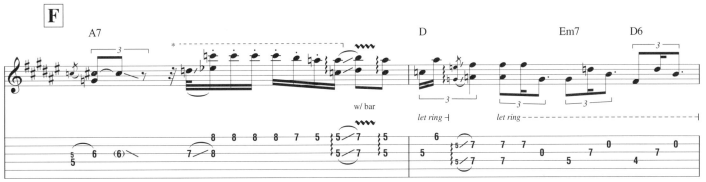

*Played as straight sixteenth-notes.

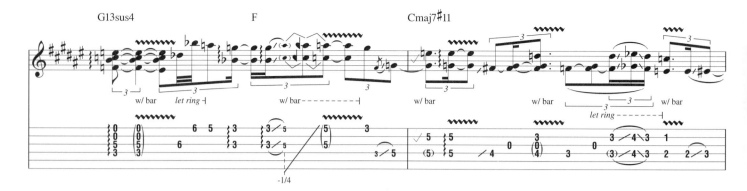

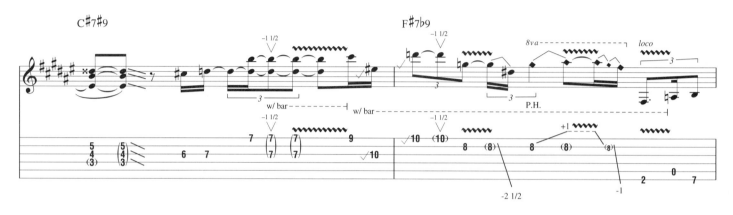

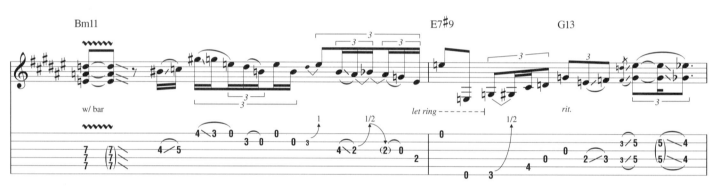

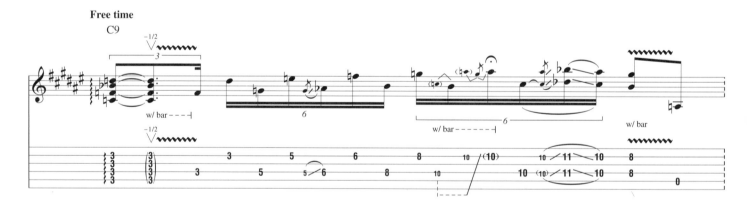

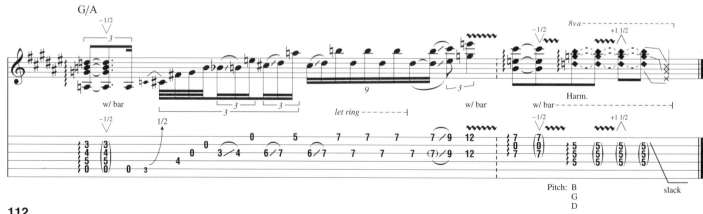

Tore Down House

Written by Scott Henderson

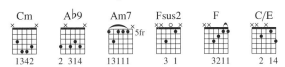

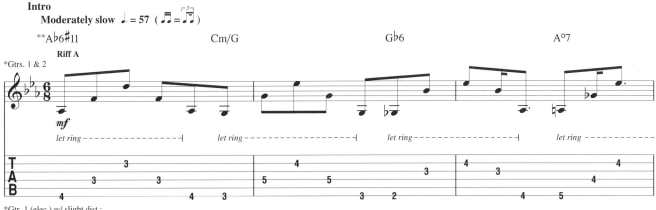

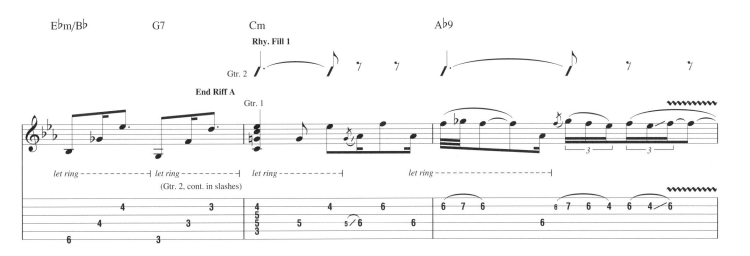

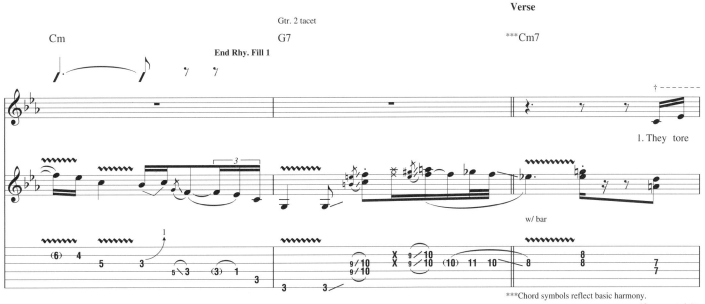

***Chord symbols reflect basic harmony.

†Sung as straight sixteenth-notes.

Fm7

down the whole house, __ ba - by,   ain't _____

w/ bar

let ring - - - ┤

Cm7

noth - ing, _____

noth - ing __ but a patch of land. __

*Played as straight
sixteenth-notes.

Fm7

They tore down __ my whole   house, __

w/ bar   w/ bar

let ring - - - - - - - - - ┤

Cm7

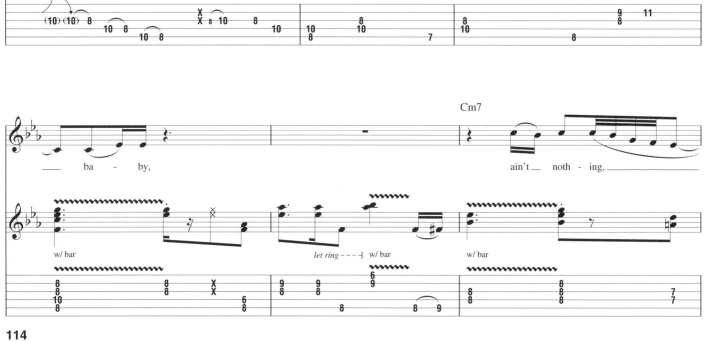

__ ba - by,   ain't noth - ing, _____

w/ bar   let ring - - - ┤ w/ bar   w/ bar

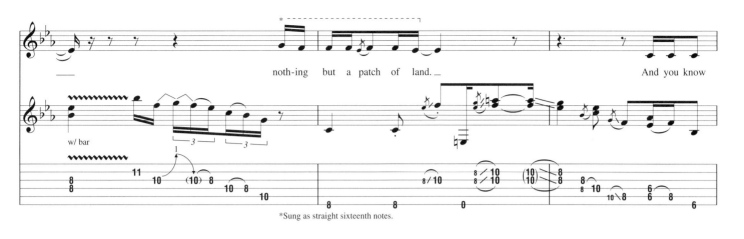

*Sung as straight sixteenth notes.

Gtrs. 1 & 2: w/ Riff A (1st 3 meas.)

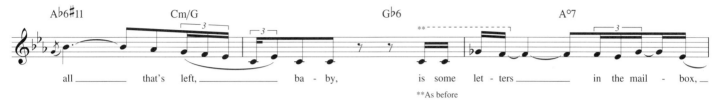

**As before

Interlude

Gtr. 2: w/ Rhy. Fill 1

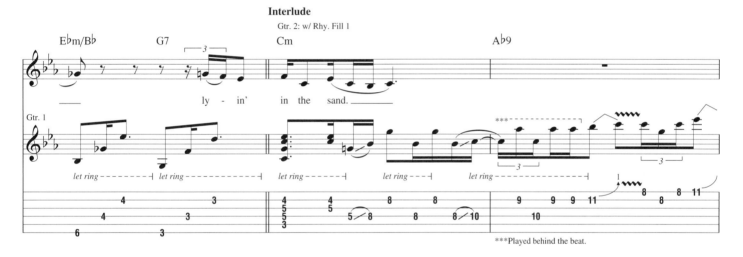

***Played behind the beat.

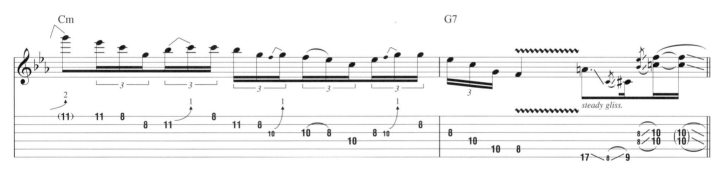

Verse

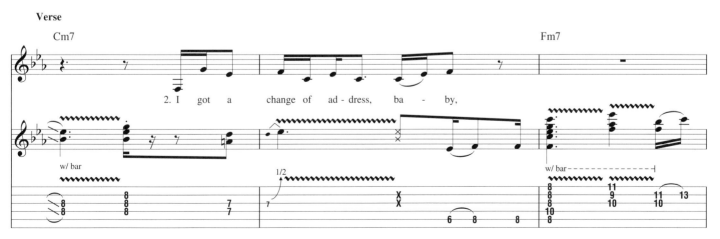

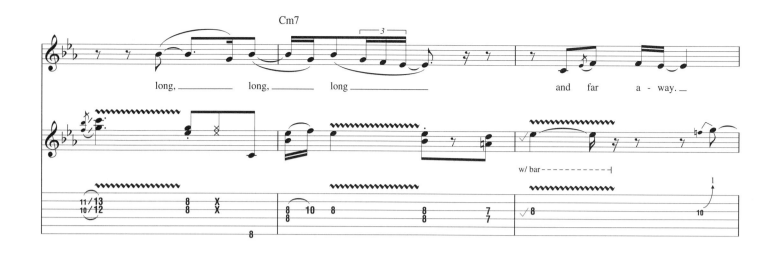

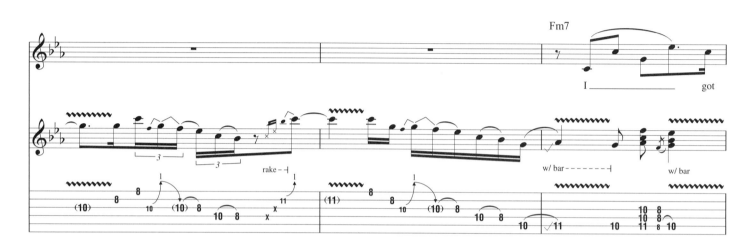

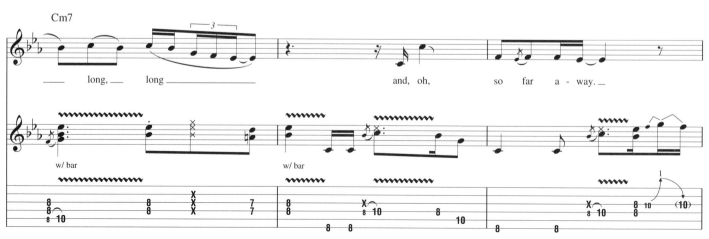

116

Guitar Solo

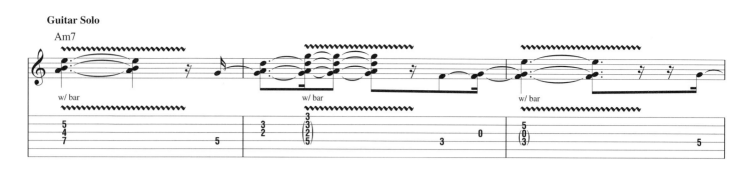

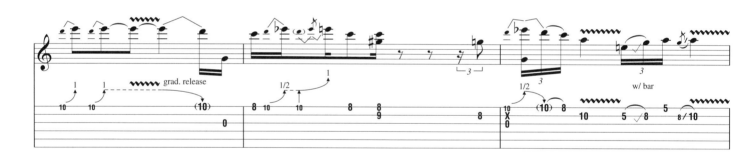

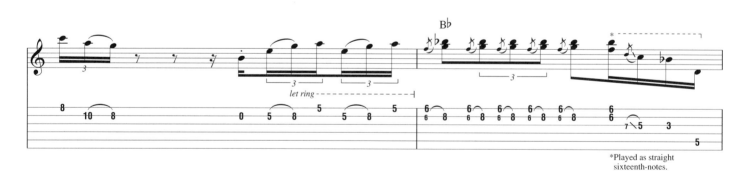

*Played as straight
sixteenth-notes.

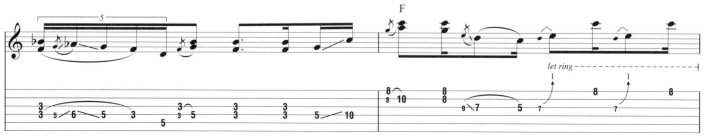

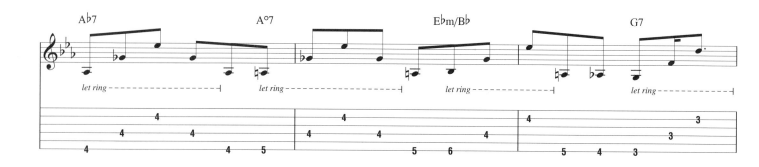

Ah, _____ hey, _____ yeah. _____

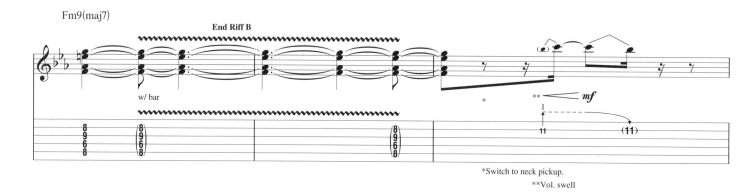

*Switch to neck pickup.
**Vol. swell

Guitar Solo

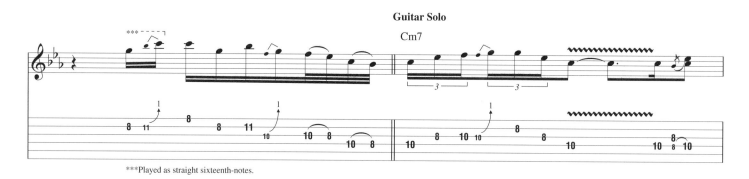

***Played as straight sixteenth-notes.

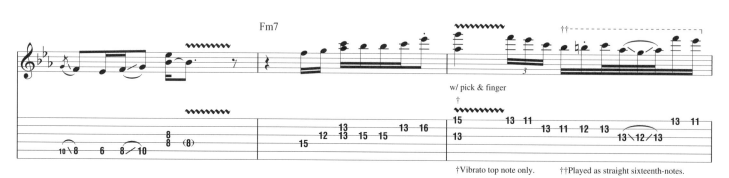

†Vibrato top note only.   ††Played as straight sixteenth-notes.

Cm7

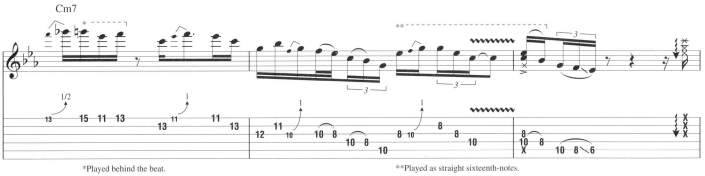

*Played behind the beat.   **Played as straight sixteenth-notes.

Fm7

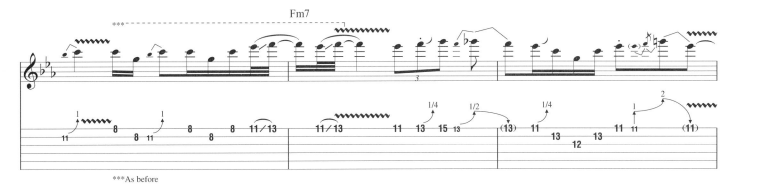

***As before

Cm7

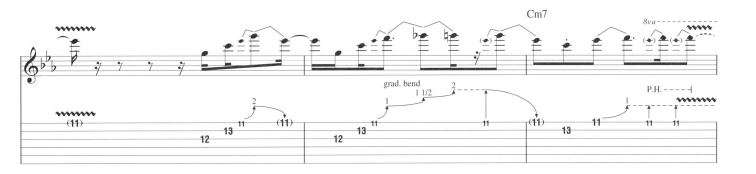

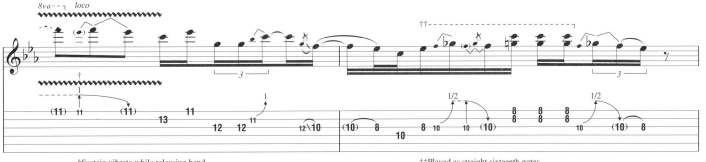

†Sustain vibrato while releasing bend.   ††Played as straight sixteenth-notes.

A♭6♯11   Cm7/G

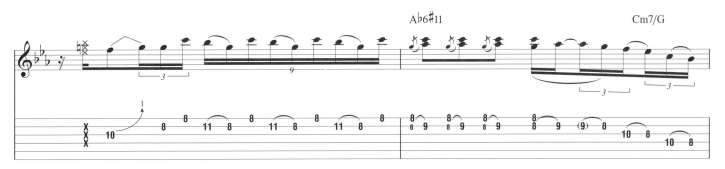

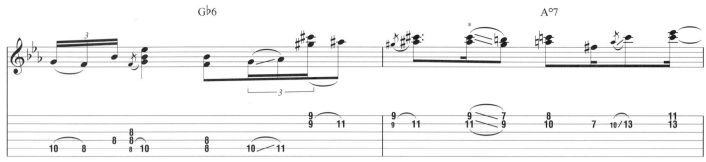

*Played as straight sixteenth-note.

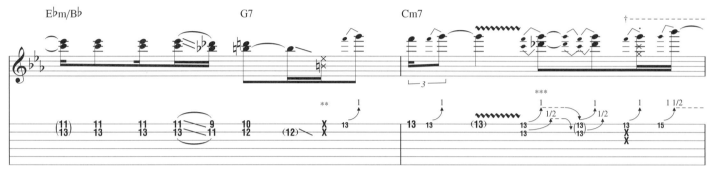

**Switch to bridge pickup.

***2nd string caught under bend finger.

†Played as straight
sixteenth-notes.

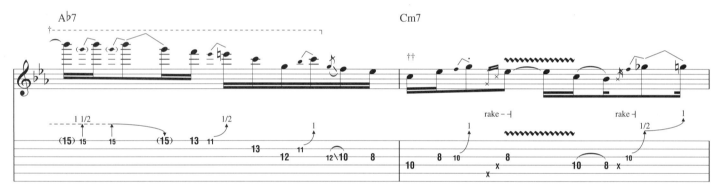

††Played as straight sixteenth notes, next 9 meas.

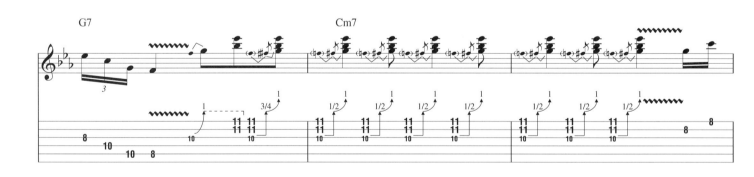

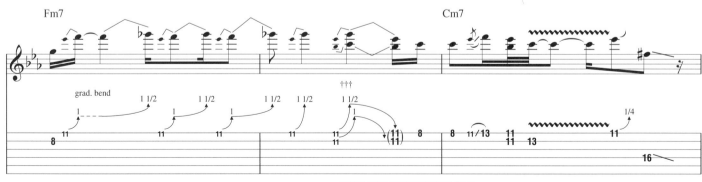

†††2nd string caught under bend finger.

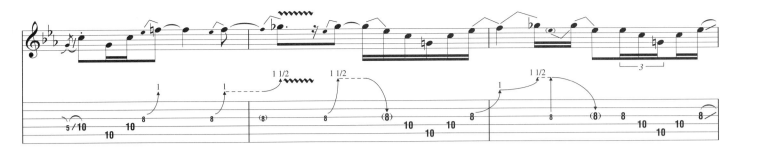

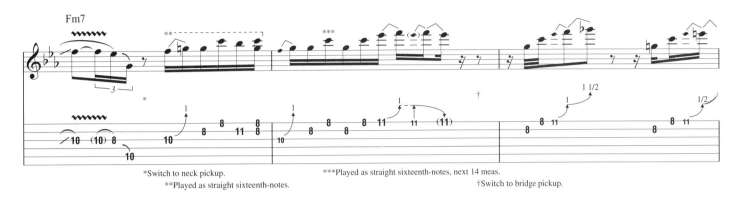

*Switch to neck pickup.
**Played as straight sixteenth-notes.
***Played as straight sixteenth-notes, next 14 meas.
†Switch to bridge pickup.

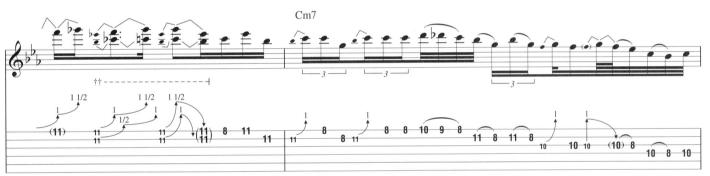

††2nd string caught under bend finger.

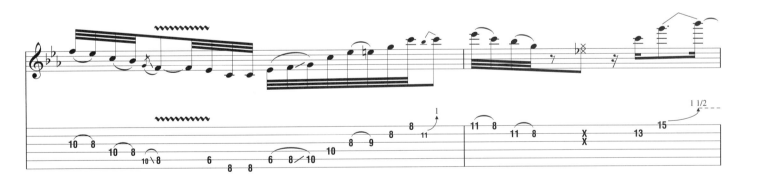

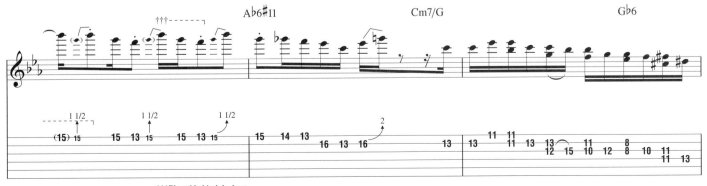

†††Played behind the beat.

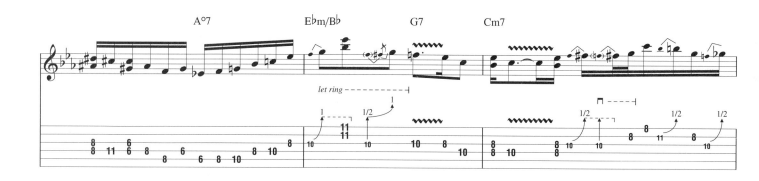

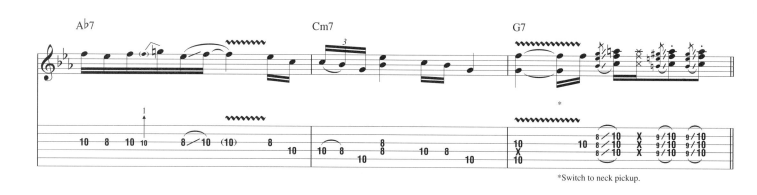

*Switch to neck pickup.

Verse

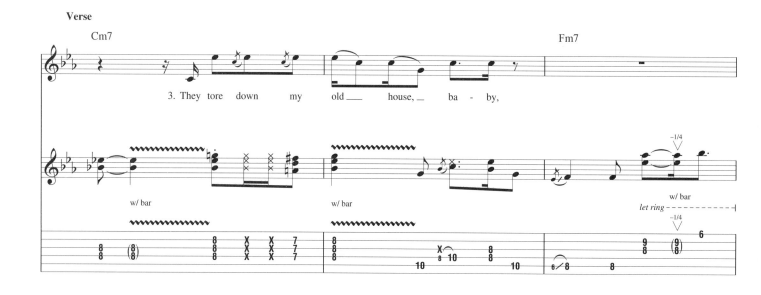

3. They tore down my old __ house, __ ba - by,

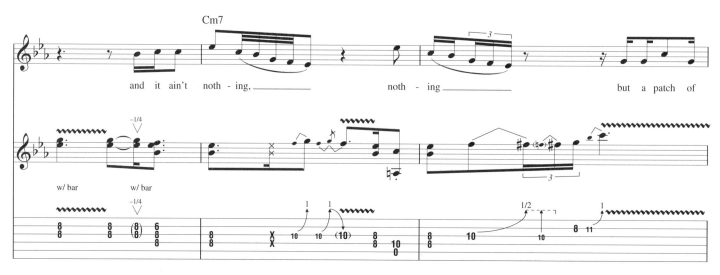

and it ain't noth - ing, __ noth - ing __ but a patch of

ba - by,   is some let - ters   in the mail - box ___ ly - ing in the

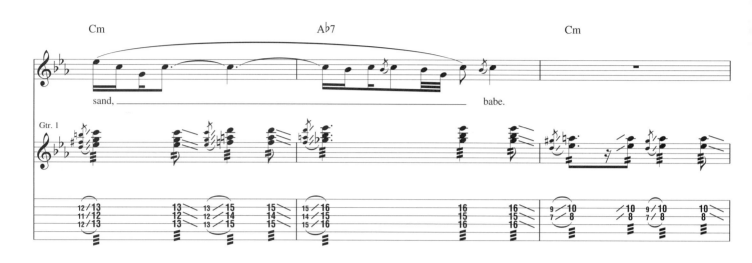

sand, ___   babe.

Gtr. 1

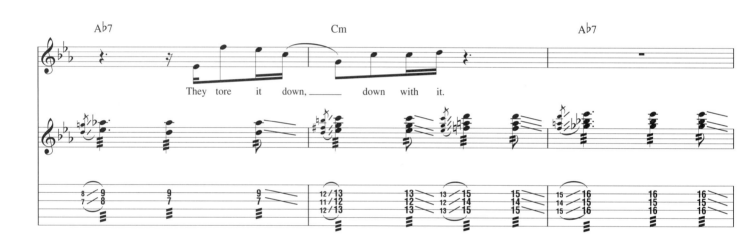

They tore it down, ___ down with it.

Gtr. 1: w/ Riff B

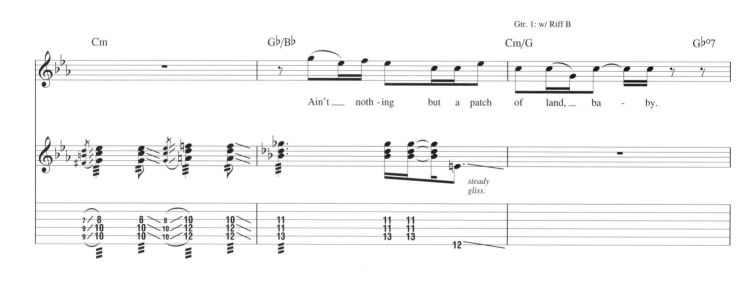

Ain't ___ noth - ing   but a patch of land, ___ ba - by.

steady
gliss.

Oh. ___   Oo.

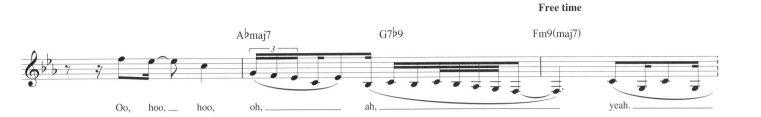

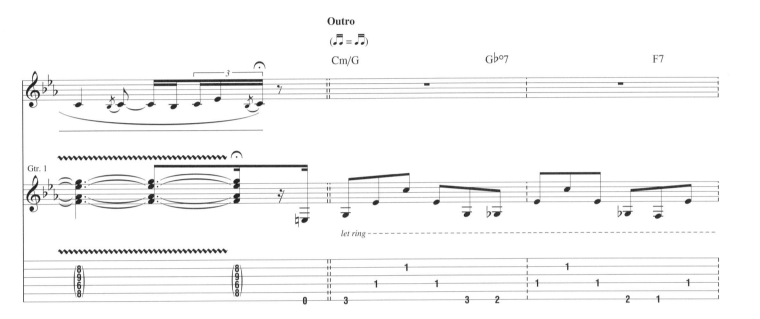

127

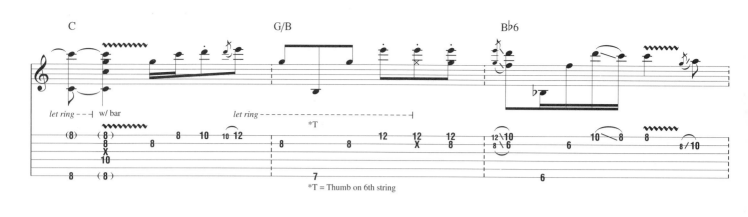

*T = Thumb on 6th string

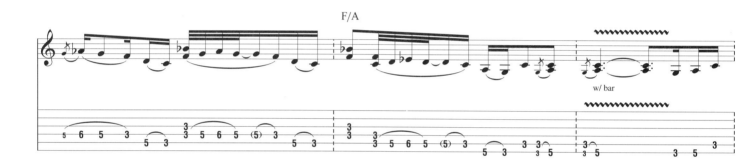

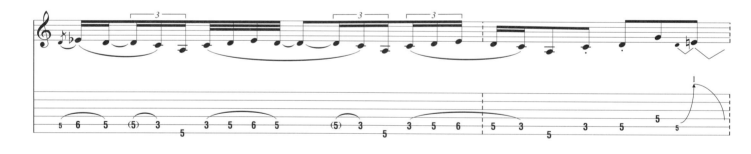

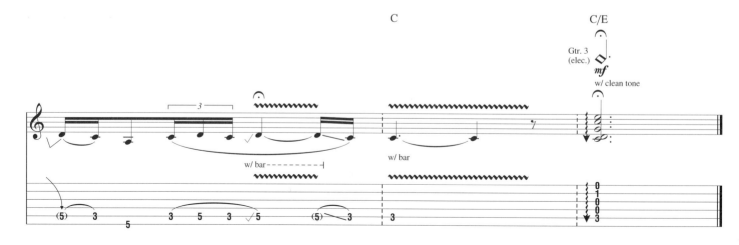

from *Well to the Bone*

Well to the Bone

Written by Scott Henderson

Tune down 1/2 step:
(low to high) Eb-Ab-Db-Gb-Bb-Eb

Intro
Moderately ♩ = 100

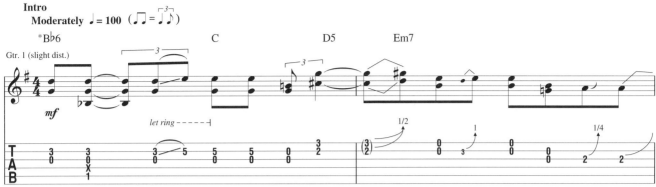

*Chord symbols reflect overall harmony.

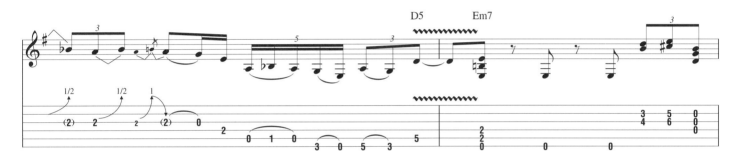

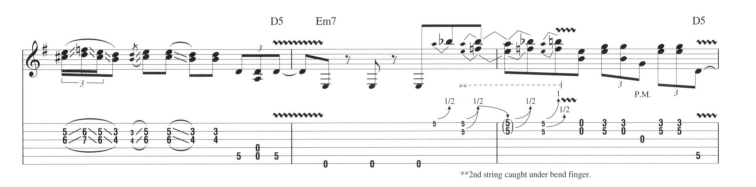

Verse

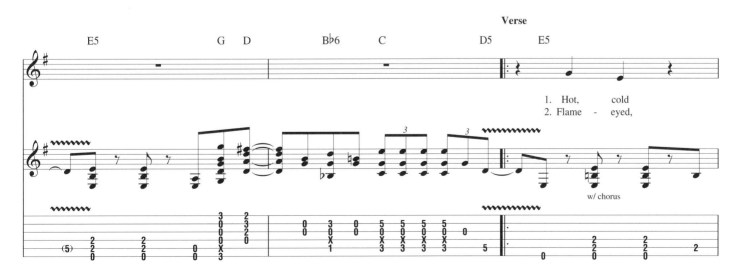

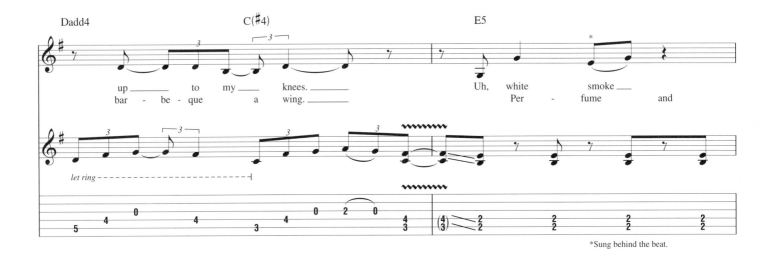

*Sung behind the beat.

2nd time, Gtr. 1: w/ Fill 1

**As before   ***As before

𝄋 **Chorus**

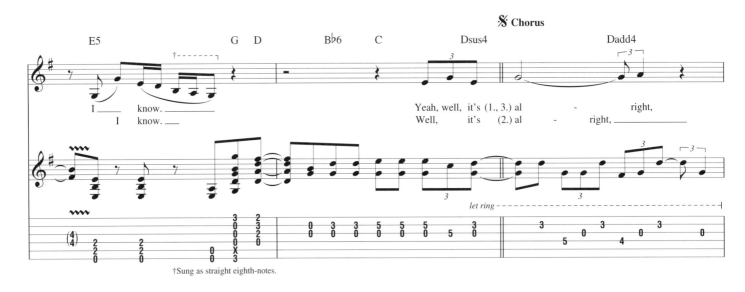

†Sung as straight eighth-notes.

Fill 1
Gtr. 1

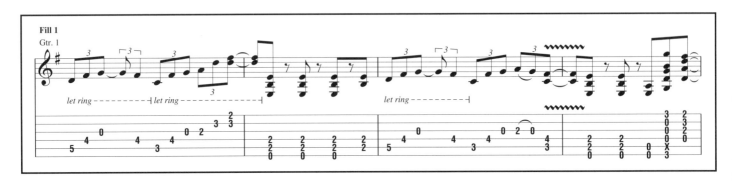

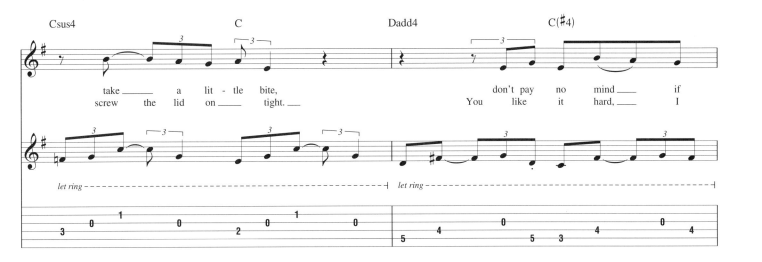

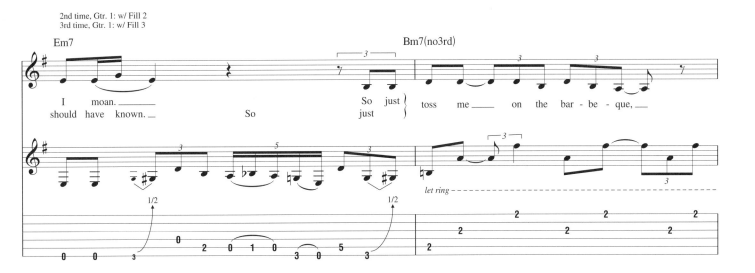

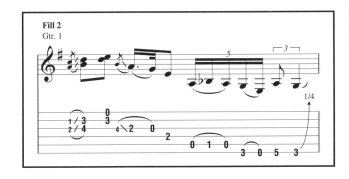

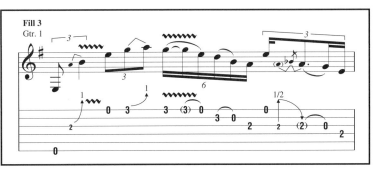

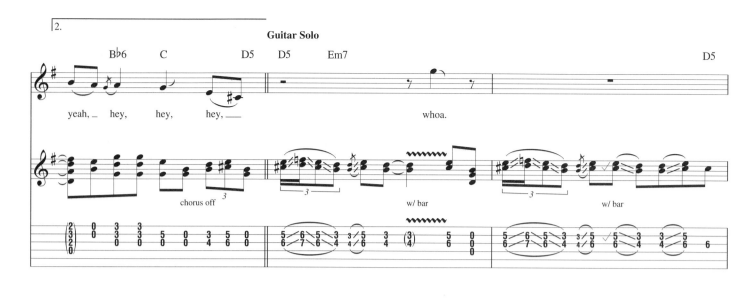

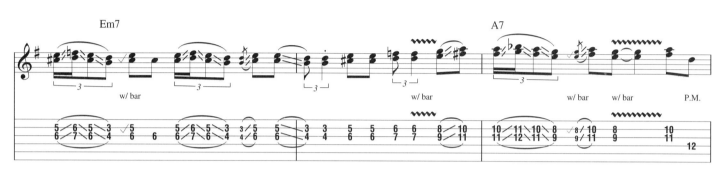

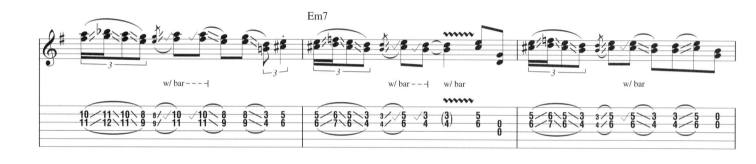

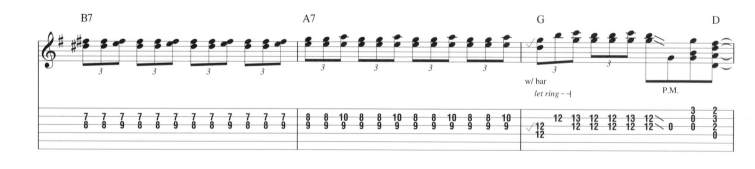

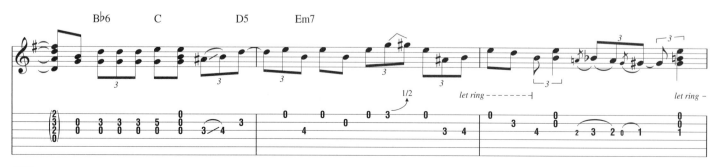

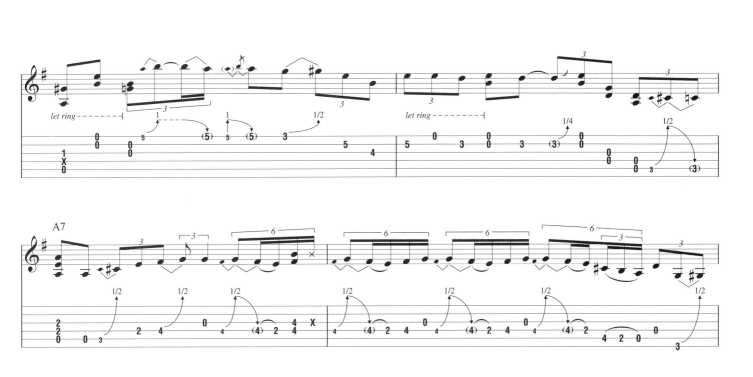

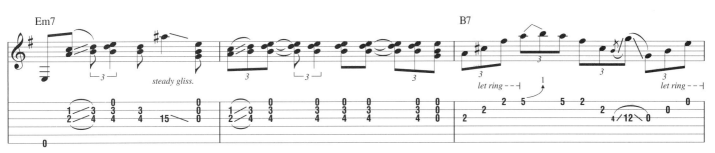

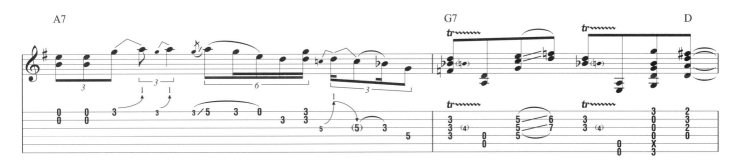

*3rd string caught under bend finger.   **Played behind the beat.

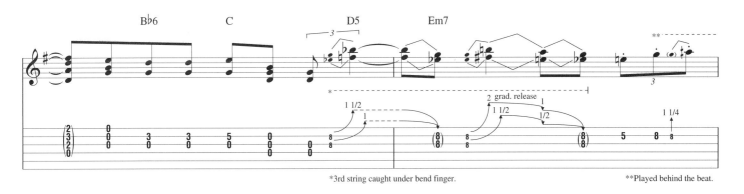

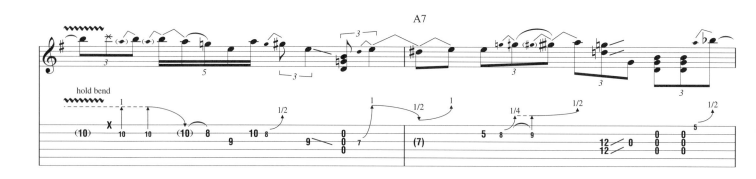

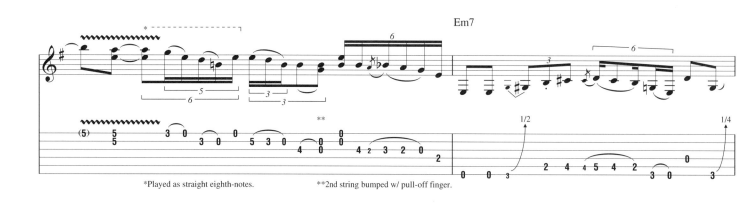

*Played as straight eighth-notes.   **2nd string bumped w/ pull-off finger.

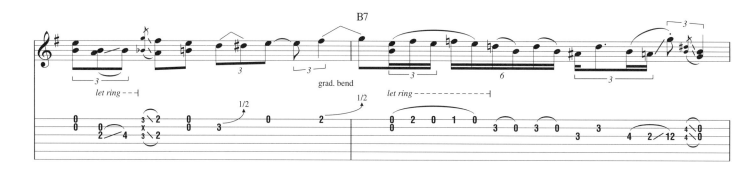

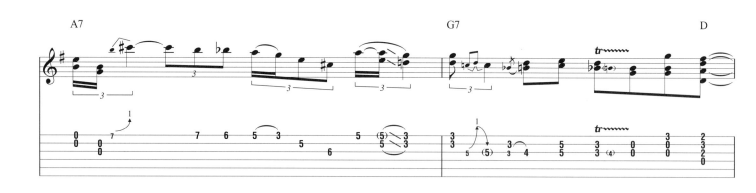

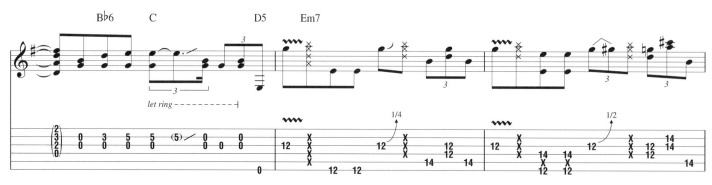

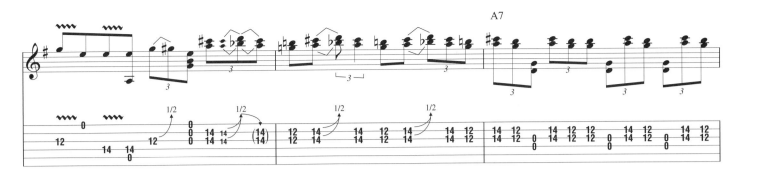

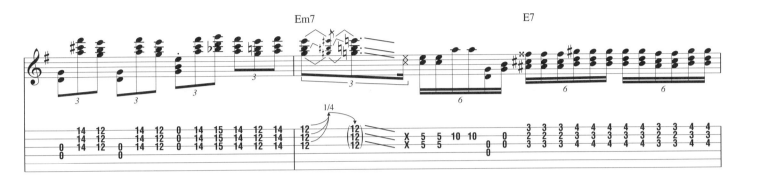

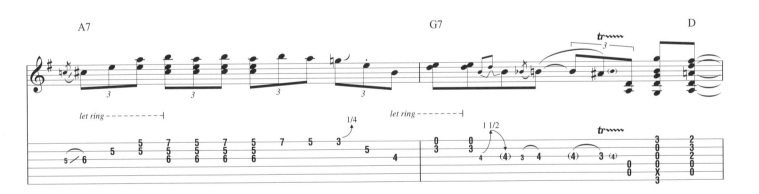

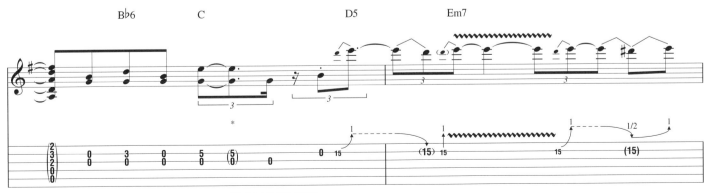

*Switch to bridge pickup.

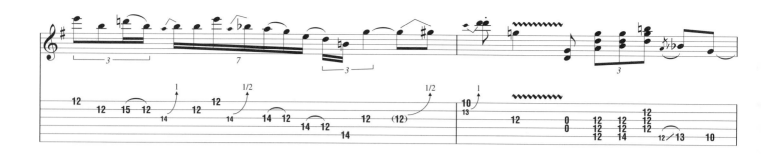

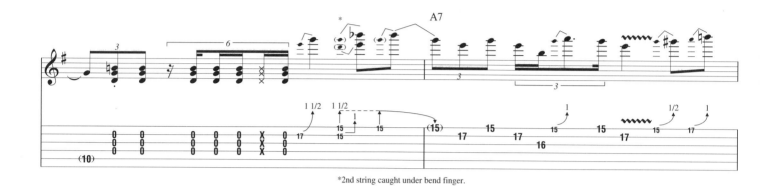

*2nd string caught under bend finger.

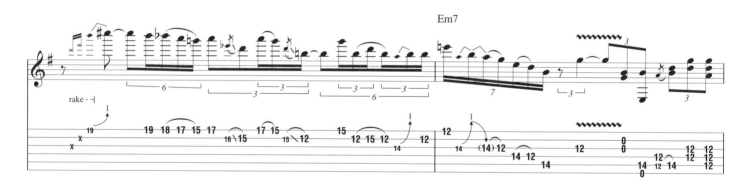

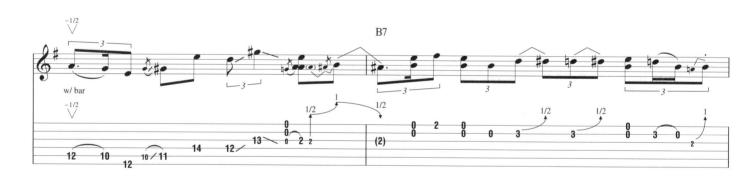

D.S. al Coda

Yeah,   it's

Guitar Notation Legend

Guitar music can be notated three different ways: on a *musical staff*, in *tablature*, and in *rhythm slashes*.

RHYTHM SLASHES are written above the staff. Strum chords in the rhythm indicated. Use the chord diagrams found at the top of the first page of the transcription for the appropriate chord voicings. Round noteheads indicate single notes.

THE MUSICAL STAFF shows pitches and rhythms and is divided by bar lines into measures. Pitches are named after the first seven letters of the alphabet.

TABLATURE graphically represents the guitar fingerboard. Each horizontal line represents a string, and each number represents a fret.

Definitions for Special Guitar Notation

HALF-STEP BEND: Strike the note and bend up 1/2 step.

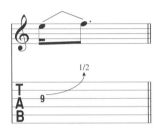

WHOLE-STEP BEND: Strike the note and bend up one step.

GRACE NOTE BEND: Strike the note and immediately bend up as indicated.

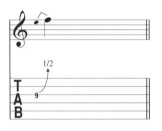

SLIGHT (MICROTONE) BEND: Strike the note and bend up 1/4 step.

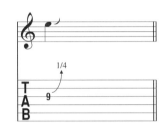

BEND AND RELEASE: Strike the note and bend up as indicated, then release back to the original note. Only the first note is struck.

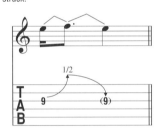

PRE-BEND: Bend the note as indicated, then strike it.

PRE-BEND AND RELEASE: Bend the note as indicated. Strike it and release the bend back to the original note.

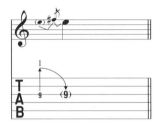

UNISON BEND: Strike the two notes simultaneously and bend the lower note up to the pitch of the higher.

VIBRATO: The string is vibrated by rapidly bending and releasing the note with the fretting hand.

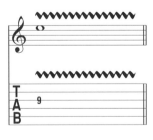

WIDE VIBRATO: The pitch is varied to a greater degree by vibrating with the fretting hand.

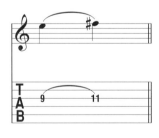

HAMMER-ON: Strike the first (lower) note with one finger, then sound the higher note (on the same string) with another finger by fretting it without picking.

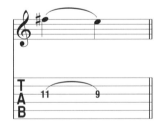

PULL-OFF: Place both fingers on the notes to be sounded. Strike the first note and without picking, pull the finger off to sound the second (lower) note.

LEGATO SLIDE: Strike the first note and then slide the same fret-hand finger up or down to the second note. The second note is not struck.

SHIFT SLIDE: Same as legato slide, except the second note is struck.

TRILL: Very rapidly alternate between the notes indicated by continuously hammering on and pulling off.

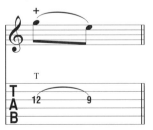

TAPPING: Hammer ("tap") the fret indicated with the pick-hand index or middle finger and pull off to the note fretted by the fret hand.

138

NATURAL HARMONIC: Strike the note while the fret-hand lightly touches the string directly over the fret indicated.

PINCH HARMONIC: The note is fretted normally and a harmonic is produced by adding the edge of the thumb or the tip of the index finger of the pick hand to the normal pick attack.

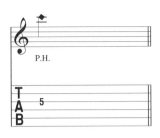

HARP HARMONIC: The note is fretted normally and a harmonic is produced by gently resting the pick hand's index finger directly above the indicated fret (in parentheses) while the pick hand's thumb or pick assists by plucking the appropriate string.

PICK SCRAPE: The edge of the pick is rubbed down (or up) the string, producing a scratchy sound.

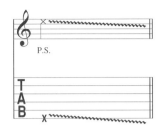

MUFFLED STRINGS: A percussive sound is produced by laying the fret hand across the string(s) without depressing, and striking them with the pick hand.

PALM MUTING: The note is partially muted by the pick hand lightly touching the string(s) just before the bridge.

RAKE: Drag the pick across the strings indicated with a single motion.

TREMOLO PICKING: The note is picked as rapidly and continuously as possible.

ARPEGGIATE: Play the notes of the chord indicated by quickly rolling them from bottom to top.

VIBRATO BAR DIVE AND RETURN: The pitch of the note or chord is dropped a specified number of steps (in rhythm), then returned to the original pitch.

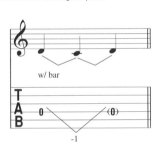

VIBRATO BAR SCOOP: Depress the bar just before striking the note, then quickly release the bar.

VIBRATO BAR DIP: Strike the note and then immediately drop a specified number of steps, then release back to the original pitch.

Additional Musical Definitions

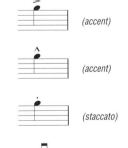

(accent)	• Accentuate note (play it louder).	
(accent)	• Accentuate note with great intensity.	
(staccato)	• Play the note short.	
	• Downstroke	
V	• Upstroke	
D.S. al Coda	• Go back to the sign (%), then play until the measure marked "*To Coda*," then skip to the section labelled "**Coda.**"	
D.C. al Fine	• Go back to the beginning of the song and play until the measure marked "*Fine*" (end).	

Rhy. Fig. • Label used to recall a recurring accompaniment pattern (usually chordal).

Riff • Label used to recall composed, melodic lines (usually single notes) which recur.

Fill • Label used to identify a brief melodic figure which is to be inserted into the arrangement.

Rhy. Fill • A chordal version of a Fill.

tacet • Instrument is silent (drops out).

• Repeat measures between signs.

• When a repeated section has different endings, play the first ending only the first time and the second ending only the second time.

NOTE: Tablature numbers in parentheses mean:
1. The note is being sustained over a system (note in standard notation is tied), or
2. The note is sustained, but a new articulation (such as a hammer-on, pull-off, slide or vibrato) begins, or
3. The note is a barely audible "ghost" note (note in standard notation is also in parentheses).

GUITAR RECORDED VERSIONS®

RECORDED VERSIONS GUITAR®

AUTHENTIC TRANSCRIPTIONS WITH NOTES AND TABLATURE

Guitar Recorded Versions® are note-for-note transcriptions of guitar music taken directly off recordings. This series, one of the most popular in print today, features some of the greatest guitar players and groups from blues and rock to country and jazz.

Guitar Recorded Versions are transcribed by the best transcribers in the business. Every book contains notes and tablature. Visit www.halleonard.com for our complete selection.

00690501 Bryan Adams – Greatest Hits $19.95
00690002 Aerosmith – Big Ones $24.95
00692015 Aerosmith – Greatest Hits $22.95
00690603 Aerosmith – O Yeah! (Ultimate Hits) $24.95
00690147 Aerosmith – Rocks $19.95
00690139 Alice in Chains $19.95
00690178 Alice in Chains – Acoustic $19.95
00694865 Alice in Chains – Dirt $19.95
00660225 Alice in Chains – Facelift $19.95
00694925 Alice in Chains – Jar of Flies/Sap $19.95
00690387 Alice in Chains – Nothing Safe: Best of the Box $19.95
00690899 All That Remains – The Fall of Ideals $19.95
00690812 All-American Rejects – Move Along $19.95
00694932 Allman Brothers Band – Definitive Collection for Guitar Volume 1 .... $24.95
00694933 Allman Brothers Band – Definitive Collection for Guitar Volume 2 .... $24.95
00694934 Allman Brothers Band – Definitive Collection for Guitar Volume 3 .... $24.95
00690755 Alter Bridge – One Day Remains $19.95
00690571 Trey Anastasio $19.95
00690158 Chet Atkins – Almost Alone $19.95
00694876 Chet Atkins – Contemporary Styles $19.95
00694878 Chet Atkins – Vintage Fingerstyle $19.95
00690865 Atreyu – A Deathgrip on Yesterday $19.95
00690609 Audioslave $19.95
00690804 Audioslave – Out of Exile $19.95
00690926 Avenged Sevenfold $22.95
00690884 Audioslave – Revelations $19.95
00690820 Avenged Sevenfold – City of Evil $22.95
00694918 Randy Bachman Collection $22.95
00690366 Bad Company – Original Anthology – Book 1 .... $19.95
00690367 Bad Company – Original Anthology – Book 2 .... $19.95
00690503 Beach Boys – Very Best of $19.95
00694929 Beatles: 1962-1966 .... $24.95
00694930 Beatles: 1967-1970 .... $24.95
00690489 Beatles – 1 .... $24.95
00694880 Beatles – Abbey Road $19.95
00690110 Beatles – Book 1 (White Album) $19.95
00690111 Beatles – Book 2 (White Album) $19.95
00694832 Beatles – For Acoustic Guitar $22.95
00690137 Beatles – A Hard Day's Night $16.95
00690482 Beatles – Let It Be $17.95
00694891 Beatles – Revolver $19.95
00694914 Beatles – Rubber Soul $19.95
00694863 Beatles – Sgt. Pepper's Lonely Hearts Club Band $19.95
00690383 Beatles – Yellow Submarine $19.95
00690175 Beck – Odelay $17.95
00690632 Beck – Sea Change $19.95
00694884 Best of George Benson $19.95
00692385 Chuck Berry $19.95
00690835 Billy Talent $19.95
00690879 Billy Talent II $19.95
00690149 Black Sabbath $14.95
00690148 Black Sabbath – Master of Reality $14.95
00690142 Black Sabbath – Paranoid $14.95
00692200 Black Sabbath – We Sold Our Soul for Rock 'N' Roll $19.95
00690115 Blind Melon – Soup $19.95
00690674 blink-182 .... $19.95
00690305 blink-182 – Dude Ranch $19.95
00690389 blink-182 – Enema of the State $19.95
00690831 blink-182 – Greatest Hits $19.95
00690523 blink-182 – Take Off Your Pants and Jacket $19.95
00690028 Blue Oyster Cult – Cult Classics $19.95
00690851 James Blunt – Back to Bedlam $22.95
00690008 Bon Jovi – Cross Road $19.95
00690491 Best of David Bowie $19.95
00690583 Box Car Racer $19.95
00690873 Breaking Benjamin – Phobia $19.95
00690764 Breaking Benjamin – We Are Not Alone $19.95
00690451 Jeff Buckley Collection $24.95
00690678 Best of Kenny Burrell $19.95
00690364 Cake – Songbook $19.95
00690564 The Calling – Camino Palmero $19.95
00690261 Carter Family Collection $19.95
00690293 Best of Steven Curtis Chapman $19.95
00690043 Best of Cheap Trick $19.95
00690171 Chicago – The Definitive Guitar Collection $22.95
00690567 Charlie Christian – The Definitive Collection $19.95
00690590 Eric Clapton – Anthology $29.95
00692391 Best of Eric Clapton – 2nd Edition $22.95
00690393 Eric Clapton – Selections from Blues $19.95
00690074 Eric Clapton – Cream of Clapton $24.95
00690010 Eric Clapton – From the Cradle $19.95
00690716 Eric Clapton – Me and Mr. Johnson $19.95
00690263 Eric Clapton – Slowhand $19.95
00694873 Eric Clapton – Timepieces $19.95
00694869 Eric Clapton – Unplugged $22.95
00690415 Clapton Chronicles – Best of Eric Clapton $18.95
00694896 John Mayall/Eric Clapton – Bluesbreakers $19.95
00690162 Best of the Clash $19.95
00690828 Coheed & Cambria – Good Apollo I'm Burning Star, IV, Vol. 1: From Fear Through the Eyes of Madness $19.95
00690494 Coldplay – Parachutes $19.95
00690593 Coldplay – A Rush of Blood to the Head $19.95
00690906 Coldplay – The Singles & B-Sides $24.95
00690806 Coldplay – X & Y $19.95
00694940 Counting Crows – August & Everything After $19.95
00690405 Counting Crows – This Desert Life $19.95
00694840 Cream – Disraeli Gears $19.95
00690838 Cream – Royal Albert Hall: London May 2-3-5-6 2005 .... $22.95
00690285 Cream – Those Were the Days $17.95
00690856 Creed – Greatest Hits $22.95
00690401 Creed – Human Clay $19.95
00690352 Creed – My Own Prison $19.95
00690551 Creed – Weathered $19.95
00690819 Best of Creedence Clearwater Revival $19.95
00690572 Steve Cropper – Soul Man $19.95
00690613 Best of Crosby, Stills & Nash $19.95
00690777 Crossfade $19.95
00699521 The Cure – Greatest Hits $24.95
00690637 Best of Dick Dale $19.95
00690882 Dashboard Confessional – Dusk and Summer $19.95
00690892 Daughtry $19.95
00690184 dc Talk – Jesus Freak $19.95
00690822 Best of Alex De Grassi $19.95
00690289 Best of Deep Purple $17.95
00690784 Best of Def Leppard $19.95
00694831 Derek and the Dominos – Layla & Other Assorted Love Songs $19.95
00690384 Best of Ani DiFranco $19.95
00690322 Ani DiFranco – Little Plastic Castle $19.95
00690191 Dire Straits – Money for Nothing $24.95
00695382 Very Best of Dire Straits – Sultans of Swing $19.95
00690347 The Doors – Anthology $22.95
00690348 The Doors – Essential Guitar Collection $16.95
00690915 Dragonforce – Inhuman Rampage $29.95
00690250 Best of Duane Eddy $16.95
00690533 Electric Light Orchestra Guitar Collection $19.95
00690909 Best of Tommy Emmanuel $19.95
00690555 Best of Melissa Etheridge $19.95
00690524 Melissa Etheridge – Skin $19.95
00690496 Best of Everclear $19.95
00690515 Extreme II – Pornograffitti $19.95
00690810 Fall Out Boy – From Under the Cork Tree $19.95
00690897 Fall Out Boy – Infinity on High $22.95
00690664 Best of Fleetwood Mac $19.95
00690870 Flyleaf $19.95
00690257 John Fogerty – Blue Moon Swamp $19.95
00690235 Foo Fighters – The Colour and the Shape $19.95
00690808 Foo Fighters – In Your Honor $19.95
00690595 Foo Fighters – One by One $19.95
00690394 Foo Fighters – There Is Nothing Left to Lose $19.95
00690805 Best of Robben Ford $19
00690842 Best of Peter Frampton $19
00690734 Franz Ferdinand $19
00694920 Best of Free $19
00690222 G3 Live – Joe Satriani, Steve Vai, and Eric Johnson $22
00694807 Danny Gatton – 88 Elmira St $19
00690438 Genesis Guitar Anthology $19
00690753 Best of Godsmack $19
00120167 Godsmack $19
00690848 Godsmack – IV $19
00690338 Goo Goo Dolls – Dizzy Up the Girl $19
00690576 Goo Goo Dolls – Gutterflower $19
00690773 Good Charlotte – Chronicles of Life and Death $19
00690601 Good Charlotte – The Young and the Hopeless $19
00690117 John Gorka Collection $19
00690591 Patty Griffin – Guitar Collection $19
00690114 Buddy Guy Collection Vol. A-J $22
00690193 Buddy Guy Collection Vol. L-Y $22
00690697 Best of Jim Hall $19
00690840 Ben Harper – Both Sides of the Gun $19
00694798 George Harrison Anthology $19
00690778 Hawk Nelson – Letters to the President $19
00690068 Return of the Hellecasters $19
00692930 Jimi Hendrix – Are You Experienced? $24
00692931 Jimi Hendrix – Axis: Bold As Love $22
00690304 Jimi Hendrix – Band of Gypsys $22
00690321 Jimi Hendrix – BBC Sessions $22
00690608 Jimi Hendrix – Blue Wild Angel $24
00694944 Jimi Hendrix – Blues $24
00692932 Jimi Hendrix – Electric Ladyland $24
00660099 Jimi Hendrix – Radio One $24
00690602 Jimi Hendrix – Smash Hits $19
00690017 Jimi Hendrix – Woodstock $24
00690843 H.I.M. – Dark Light .... $19.
00690869 Hinder – Extreme Behavior $19
00660029 Buddy Holly .... $19.
00660169 John Lee Hooker – A Blues Legend .... $19.
00694905 Howlin' Wolf $19
00690692 Very Best of Billy Idol .... $19.
00690688 Incubus – A Crow Left of the Murder .... $19.
00690457 Incubus – Make Yourself .... $19.
00690544 Incubus – Morningview .... $19.
00690136 Indigo Girls – 1200 Curfews .... $22.
00690790 Iron Maiden Anthology .... $24.
00690887 Iron Maiden – A Matter of Life and Death .... $19.
00690730 Alan Jackson – Guitar Collection .... $19.
00694938 Elmore James – Master Electric Slide Guitar .... $19.
00690652 Best of Jane's Addiction .... $19.
00690721 Jet – Get Born .... $19.
00690684 Jethro Tull – Aqualung .... $19.
00690647 Best of Jewel .... $19.
00694833 Billy Joel for Guitar .... $19.
00690898 John 5 – The Devil Knows My Name .... $22.
00690814 John 5 – Songs for Sanity .... $19.
00690751 John 5 – Vertigo .... $19.
00694912 Eric Johnson – Ah Via Musicom .... $19.
00690660 Best of Eric Johnson .... $19.
00690845 Eric Johnson – Bloom .... $19.
00690169 Eric Johnson – Venus Isle .... $22.
00690846 Jack Johnson and Friends – Sing-A-Longs and Lullabie for the Film Curious George .... $19.
00690271 Robert Johnson – The New Transcriptions .... $24.
00699131 Best of Janis Joplin .... $19.
00690427 Best of Judas Priest .... $19.
00690651 Juanes – Exitos de Juanes .... $19.
00690277 Best of Kansas .... $19.
00690742 The Killers – Hot Fuss .... $19.
00690888 The Killers – Sam's Town .... $19.
00690504 Very Best of Albert King .... $19.
00690444 B.B. King & Eric Clapton – Riding with the King .... $19.
00690134 Freddie King Collection .... $19.
00690339 Best of the Kinks .... $19.

RECORDED VERSIONS GUITAR®

AUTHENTIC TRANSCRIPTIONS
WITH NOTES AND TABLATURE

00690157 Kiss – Alive!	$19.95	
00694903 Best of Kiss for Guitar	$24.95	
00690164 Mark Knopfler Guitar – Vol. 1	$19.95	
00690163 Mark Knopfler/Chet Atkins – Neck and Neck	$19.95	
00690780 Korn – Greatest Hits, Volume 1	$22.95	
00690836 Korn – See You on the Other Side	$19.95	
00690377 Kris Kristofferson Collection	$17.95	
00690861 Kutless – Hearts of the Innocent	$19.95	
00690834 Lamb of God – Ashes of the Wake	$19.95	
00690875 Lamb of God – Sacrament	$19.95	
00690890 Ray LaMontagne – Till the Sun Turns Black	$19.95	
00690823 Ray LaMontagne – Trouble	$19.95	
00690658 Johnny Lang – Long Time Coming	$19.95	
00690726 Avril Lavigne – Under My Skin	$19.95	
00690679 John Lennon – Guitar Collection	$19.95	
00690279 Ottmar Liebert + Luna Negra – Opium Highlights	$19.95	
00690785 Best of Limp Bizkit	$19.95	
00690782 Linkin Park – Meteora	$22.95	
00690922 Linkin Park – Minutes to Midnight	$19.95	
00690743 Los Lonely Boys	$19.95	
00690720 Lostprophets – Start Something	$19.95	
00690525 Best of George Lynch	$19.95	
00694954 New Best of Lynyrd Skynyrd	$19.95	
00690577 Yngwie Malmsteen – Anthology	$24.95	
00694845 Yngwie Malmsteen – Fire and Ice	$19.95	
00694755 Yngwie Malmsteen's Rising Force	$19.95	
00694757 Yngwie Malmsteen – Trilogy	$19.95	
00690754 Marilyn Manson – Lest We Forget	$19.95	
00694956 Bob Marley – Legend	$19.95	
00690548 Very Best of Bob Marley & The Wailers – One Love	$19.95	
00694945 Bob Marley – Songs of Freedom	$24.95	
00690914 Maroon 5 – It Won't Be Soon Before Long	$19.95	
00690657 Maroon 5 – Songs About Jane	$19.95	
00690442 Matchbox 20 – Mad Season	$19.95	
00690239 Matchbox 20 – Yourself or Someone like You	$19.95	
00690382 Sarah McLachlan – Mirrorball	$19.95	
00694952 Megadeth – Countdown to Extinction	$19.95	
00690244 Megadeth – Cryptic Writings	$19.95	
00694951 Megadeth – Rust in Peace	$22.95	
00690011 Megadeth – Youthanasia	$19.95	
00690505 John Mellencamp Guitar Collection	$19.95	
00690562 Pat Metheny – Bright Size Life	$19.95	
00690646 Pat Metheny – One Quiet Night	$19.95	
00690559 Pat Metheny – Question & Answer	$19.95	
00690040 Steve Miller Band Greatest Hits	$19.95	
00690769 Modest Mouse – Good News for People Who Love Bad News	$19.95	
00694802 Gary Moore – Still Got the Blues	$19.95	
00690103 Alanis Morissette – Jagged Little Pill	$19.95	
00690787 Mudvayne – L.D. 50	$22.95	
00690500 Ricky Nelson Guitar Collection	$17.95	
00690722 New Found Glory – Catalyst	$19.95	
00690880 New Found Glory – Coming Home	$19.95	
00690345 Best of Newsboys	$17.95	
00690924 The Nightwatchman – One Man Revolution	$19.95	
00690611 Nirvana	$22.95	
00694895 Nirvana – Bleach	$19.95	
00690189 Nirvana – From the Muddy Banks of the Wishkah	$19.95	
00694913 Nirvana – In Utero	$19.95	
00694901 Nirvana – Incesticide	$19.95	
00694883 Nirvana – Nevermind	$19.95	
00690026 Nirvana – Unplugged in New York	$19.95	
00120112 No Doubt – Tragic Kingdom	$22.95	
00690121 Oasis – (What's the Story) Morning Glory	$19.95	
00690226 Oasis – The Other Side of Oasis	$19.95	
00690358 The Offspring – Americana	$19.95	
00690485 The Offspring – Conspiracy of One	$19.95	
00690204 The Offspring – Ixnay on the Hombre	$17.95	
00690203 The Offspring – Smash	$18.95	
00690818 The Best of Opeth	$22.95	

00694847 Best of Ozzy Osbourne	$22.95	
00690921 Ozzy Osbourne – Black Rain	$19.95	
00694830 Ozzy Osbourne – No More Tears	$19.95	
00690399 Ozzy Osbourne – The Ozzman Cometh	$19.95	
00690129 Ozzy Osbourne – Ozzmosis	$22.95	
00690866 Panic! At the Disco – A Fever You Can't Sweat Out	$19.95	
00690885 Papa Roach – The Paramour Sessions	$19.95	
00690594 Best of Les Paul	$19.95	
00690546 P.O.D. – Satellite	$19.95	
00694855 Pearl Jam – Ten	$19.95	
00690439 A Perfect Circle – Mer De Noms	$19.95	
00690661 A Perfect Circle – Thirteenth Step	$19.95	
00690499 Tom Petty – Definitive Guitar Collection	$19.95	
00690868 Tom Petty – Highway Companion	$19.95	
00690176 Phish – Billy Breathes	$22.95	
00690240 Phish – Hoist	$19.95	
00690331 Phish – Story of the Ghost	$19.95	
00690428 Pink Floyd – Dark Side of the Moon	$19.95	
00690789 Best of Poison	$19.95	
00693864 Best of The Police	$19.95	
00690299 Best of Elvis: The King of Rock 'n' Roll	$19.95	
00692535 Elvis Presley	$19.95	
00690003 Classic Queen	$24.95	
00694975 Queen – Greatest Hits	$24.95	
00690670 Very Best of Queensryche	$19.95	
00690878 The Raconteurs – Broken Boy Soldiers	$19.95	
00694910 Rage Against the Machine	$19.95	
00690145 Rage Against the Machine – Evil Empire	$19.95	
00690179 Rancid – And Out Come the Wolves	$22.95	
00690426 Best of Ratt	$19.95	
00690055 Red Hot Chili Peppers – Blood Sugar Sex Magik	$19.95	
00690584 Red Hot Chili Peppers – By the Way	$19.95	
00690379 Red Hot Chili Peppers – Californication	$19.95	
00690673 Red Hot Chili Peppers – Greatest Hits	$19.95	
00690090 Red Hot Chili Peppers – One Hot Minute	$22.95	
00690852 Red Hot Chili Peppers – Stadium Arcadium	$24.95	
00690893 The Red Jumpsuit Apparatus – Don't You Fake It	$19.95	
00690511 Django Reinhardt – The Definitive Collection	$19.95	
00690779 Relient K – MMHMM	$19.95	
00690643 Relient K – Two Lefts Don't Make a Right ... But Three Do	$19.95	
00694899 R.E.M. – Automatic for the People	$19.95	
00690260 Jimmie Rodgers Guitar Collection	$19.95	
00690014 Rolling Stones – Exile on Main Street	$24.95	
00690631 Rolling Stones – Guitar Anthology	$24.95	
00690685 David Lee Roth – Eat 'Em and Smile	$19.95	
00690031 Santana's Greatest Hits	$19.95	
00690796 Very Best of Michael Schenker	$19.95	
00690566 Best of Scorpions	$19.95	
00690604 Bob Seger – Guitar Anthology	$19.95	
00690659 Bob Seger and the Silver Bullet Band – Greatest Hits, Volume 2	$17.95	
00690896 Shadows Fall – Threads of Life	$19.95	
00690803 Best of Kenny Wayne Shepherd Band	$19.95	
00690750 Kenny Wayne Shepherd – The Place You're In	$19.95	
00690857 Shinedown – Us and Them	$19.95	
00690196 Silverchair – Freak Show	$19.95	
00690130 Silverchair – Frogstomp	$19.95	
00690872 Slayer – Christ Illusion	$19.95	
00690419 Slipknot	$19.95	
00690530 Slipknot – Iowa	$19.95	
00690733 Slipknot – Volume 3 (The Subliminal Verses)	$19.95	
00690330 Social Distortion – Live at the Roxy	$19.95	
00120004 Best of Steely Dan	$24.95	
00694921 Best of Steppenwolf	$22.95	
00690655 Best of Mike Stern	$19.95	
00694801 Best of Rod Stewart	$22.95	
00690021 Sting – Fields of Gold	$19.95	
00690597 Stone Sour	$19.95	
00690689 Story of the Year – Page Avenue	$19.95	
00690520 Styx Guitar Collection	$19.95	
00120081 Sublime	$19.95	

00690519 SUM 41 – All Killer No Filler	$19.95	
00690767 Switchfoot – The Beautiful Letdown	$19.95	
00690425 System of a Down	$19.95	
00690830 System of a Down – Hypnotize	$19.95	
00690799 System of a Down – Mezmerize	$19.95	
00690531 System of a Down – Toxicity	$19.95	
00694824 Best of James Taylor	$16.95	
00694887 Best of Thin Lizzy	$19.95	
00690825 Third Day – Wherever You Are	$19.95	
00690671 Three Days Grace	$19.95	
00690871 Three Days Grace – One-X	$19.95	
00690737 3 Doors Down – The Better Life	$22.95	
00690776 3 Doors Down – Seventeen Days	$19.95	
00690891 30 Seconds to Mars – A Beautiful Lie	$19.95	
00690269 311 – Grass Roots	$19.95	
00690665 Thursday – War All the Time	$19.95	
00690030 Toad the Wet Sprocket	$19.95	
00690654 Best of Train	$19.95	
00690683 Robin Trower – Bridge of Sighs	$19.95	
00699191 U2 – Best of: 1980-1990	$19.95	
00690732 U2 – Best of: 1990-2000	$19.95	
00690894 U2 – 18 Singles	$19.95	
00690775 U2 – How to Dismantle an Atomic Bomb	$22.95	
00690039 Steve Vai – Alien Love Secrets	$24.95	
00690172 Steve Vai – Fire Garden	$24.95	
00660137 Steve Vai – Passion & Warfare	$24.95	
00690881 Steve Vai – Real Illusions: Reflections	$24.95	
00694904 Steve Vai – Sex and Religion	$24.95	
00690392 Steve Vai – The Ultra Zone	$19.95	
00690024 Stevie Ray Vaughan – Couldn't Stand the Weather	$19.95	
00690370 Stevie Ray Vaughan and Double Trouble – The Real Deal: Greatest Hits Volume 2	$22.95	
00690116 Stevie Ray Vaughan – Guitar Collection	$24.95	
00660136 Stevie Ray Vaughan – In Step	$19.95	
00694879 Stevie Ray Vaughan – In the Beginning	$19.95	
00660058 Stevie Ray Vaughan – Lightnin' Blues '83-'87	$24.95	
00690036 Stevie Ray Vaughan – Live Alive	$24.95	
00694835 Stevie Ray Vaughan – The Sky Is Crying	$22.95	
00690025 Stevie Ray Vaughan – Soul to Soul	$19.95	
00690015 Stevie Ray Vaughan – Texas Flood	$19.95	
00694776 Vaughan Brothers – Family Style	$19.95	
00690772 Velvet Revolver – Contraband	$22.95	
00690920 Velvet Revolver – Libertad	$19.95	
00690132 The T-Bone Walker Collection	$19.95	
00694789 Muddy Waters – Deep Blues	$24.95	
00690071 Weezer (The Blue Album)	$19.95	
00690516 Weezer (The Green Album)	$19.95	
00690286 Weezer – Pinkerton	$19.95	
00690447 Best of the Who	$24.95	
00694970 The Who – Definitive Guitar Collection: A-E	$24.95	
00694971 The Who – Definitive Guitar Collection F-Li	$24.95	
00694972 The Who – Definitive Guitar Collection: Lo-R	$24.95	
00694973 The Who – Definitive Guitar Collection: S-Y	$24.95	
00690672 Best of Dar Williams	$19.95	
00690320 Dar Williams Songbook	$19.95	
00690319 Stevie Wonder – Some of the Best	$17.95	
00690596 Best of the Yardbirds	$19.95	
00690696 Yeah Yeah Yeahs – Fever to Tell	$19.95	
00690844 Yellowcard – Lights and Sounds	$19.95	
00690904 Neil Young – Harvest	$19.95	
00690443 Frank Zappa – Hot Rats	$19.95	
00690589 ZZ Top – Guitar Anthology	$22.95	

FOR MORE INFORMATION, SEE YOUR LOCAL MUSIC DEALER, OR WRITE TO:

HAL•LEONARD® CORPORATION

7777 W. BLUEMOUND RD. P.O. BOX 13819 MILWAUKEE, WI 53213

Complete songlists and more at www.halleonard.com
Prices, contents, and availability subject to change without notice.

0308

GUITAR BIBLES
from **HAL•LEONARD®**

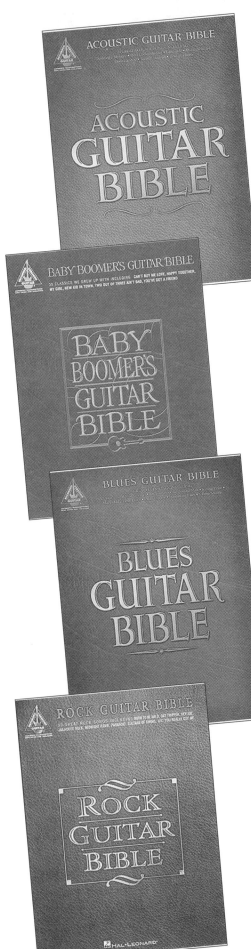

Hal Leonard proudly presents the Guitar Bible series. Each volume contains great songs in authentic, note-for-note transcriptions with lyrics and tablature.

ACOUSTIC GUITAR BIBLE
35 acoustic classics: Angie • Building a Mystery • Change the World • Dust in the Wind • Hold My Hand • Iris • Maggie May • Southern Cross • Tears in Heaven • Wild World • and more.
00690432...$19.95

ACOUSTIC ROCK GUITAR BIBLE
35 classics: And I Love Her • Behind Blue Eyes • Come to My Window • Free Fallin' • Give a Little Bit • More Than Words • Night Moves • Pink Houses • Slide • 3 AM • and more.
00690625...$19.95

BABY BOOMER'S GUITAR BIBLE
35 songs: Angie • Can't Buy Me Love • Happy Together • Hey Jude • Imagine • Laughing • Longer • My Girl • New Kid in Town • Rebel, Rebel • Wild Thing • and more.
00690412...$19.95

BLUES GUITAR BIBLE
35 blues tunes: Boom Boom • Hide Away • I Can't Quit You Baby • I'm Your Hoochie Coochie Man • Killing Floor • Pride and Joy • Sweet Little Angel • The Thrill Is Gone • and more.
00690437...$19.95

BLUES-ROCK GUITAR BIBLE
35 songs: Cross Road Blues (Crossroads) • Hide Away • The House Is Rockin' • Love Struck Baby • Move It On Over • Piece of My Heart • Statesboro Blues • You Shook Me • more.
00690450...$19.95

CLASSIC ROCK GUITAR BIBLE
33 essential rock songs: Beast of Burden • Cat Scratch Fever • Double Vision • Free Ride • Hard to Handle • Life in the Fast Lane • The Stroke • Won't Get Fooled Again • and more.
00690662...$19.95

COUNTRY GUITAR BIBLE
35 country classics: Ain't Goin' Down • Blue Eyes Crying in the Rain • Boot Scootin' Boogie • Friends in Low Places • I'm So Lonesome I Could Cry • T-R-O-U-B-L-E • and more.
00690465...$19.95

DISCO GUITAR BIBLE
30 stand-out songs from the disco days: Brick House • Disco Inferno • Funkytown • Get Down Tonight • I Love the Night Life • Le Freak • Stayin' Alive • Y.M.C.A. • and more.
00690627...$17.95

EARLY ROCK GUITAR BIBLE
35 fantastic classics: Blue Suede Shoes • Do Wah Diddy Diddy • Hang On Sloopy • I'm a Believer • Louie, Louie • Oh, Pretty Woman • Surfin' U.S.A. • Twist and Shout • and more.
00690680...$17.95

FOLK-ROCK GUITAR BIBLE
35 songs: At Seventeen • Blackbird • Fire and Rain • Happy Together • Leaving on a Jet Plane • Our House • Time in a Bottle • Turn! Turn! Turn! • You've Got a Friend • more.
00690464...$19.95

GRUNGE GUITAR BIBLE
30 songs: All Apologies • Counting Blue Cars • Glycerine • Jesus Christ Pose • Lithium • Man in the Box • Nearly Lost You • Smells like Teen Spirit • This Is a Call • Violet • and more.
00690649...$17.95

HARD ROCK GUITAR BIBLE
35 songs: Ballroom Blitz • Bang a Gong • Barracuda • Living After Midnight • Rock You like a Hurricane • School's Out • Welcome to the Jungle • You Give Love a Bad Name • more.
00690453...$19.95

INSTRUMENTAL GUITAR BIBLE
37 great instrumentals: Always with Me, Always with You • Green Onions • Hide Away • Jessica • Linus and Lucy • Perfidi • Satch Boogie • Tequila • Walk Don't Run • and more.
00690514...$19.9

JAZZ GUITAR BIBLE
31 songs: Body and Soul • In a Sentimental Mood • My Funn Valentine • Nuages • Satin Doll • So What • Star Dust • Tak Five • Tangerine • Yardbird Suite • and more.
00690466...$19.9

MODERN ROCK GUITAR BIBLE
26 rock favorites: Aerials (System of a Down) • Alive (P.O.D.) Cold Hard Bitch (Jet) • Kryptonite (3 Doors Down) • Like Stone (Audioslave) • Whatever (Godsmack) • and more.
00690724...$19.9

NÜ METAL GUITAR BIBLE
25 edgy metal hits: Aenema • Black • Edgecrusher • Last Reso • People of the Sun • Schism • Southtown • Take a Loo Around • Toxicity • Youth of the Nation • and more.
00690569...$19.9

POP/ROCK GUITAR BIBLE
35 pop hits: Change the World • Heartache Tonight • Money fo Nothing • Mony, Mony • Pink Houses • Smooth • Summer c '69 • 3 AM • What I Like About You • and more.
00690517...$19.9

R&B GUITAR BIBLE
35 R&B classics: Brick House • Fire • I Got You (I Feel Good • Love Rollercoaster • Shining Star • Sir Duke • Super Freak and more.
00690452...$19.9

ROCK GUITAR BIBLE
33 songs: All Day and All of the Night • Born to Be Wild • Da Tripper • Hey Joe • Jailhouse Rock • Money • Paranoid Sultans of Swing • Walk This Way • You Really Got Me • more
00690313...$19.9

ROCKABILLY GUITAR BIBLE
31 songs from artists such as Elvis, Buddy Holly and the Bria Setzer Orchestra: Blue Suede Shoes • Hello Mary Lou • Pegg Sue • Rock This Town • Travelin' Man • and more.
00690570...$19.9

SOUL GUITAR BIBLE
33 songs: Groovin' • I've Been Loving You Too Long • Let's G It On • My Girl • Respect • Theme from Shaft • Soul Man • a more.
00690506...$19.9

SOUTHERN ROCK GUITAR BIBLE
25 southern rock classics: Can't You See • Free Bird • Hold O Loosely • La Grange • Midnight Rider • Sweet Home Alabama and more.
00690723...$19.9

Prices, contents, and availability subject to change without notice

FOR MORE INFORMATION, SEE YOUR LOCAL MUSIC DEALER, OR WRITE TO:

HAL•LEONARD®
CORPORATION
7777 W. BLUEMOUND RD. P.O. BOX 13819 MILWAUKEE, WI 53213

Visit Hal Leonard online at **www.halleonard.com**

0600

This series will help you play your favorite songs quickly and easily. **INCLUDES TAB** Just follow the tab and listen to the CD to hear how the guitar should sound, and then play along using the separate backing tracks. Mac or PC users can also slow down the tempo without changing pitch by using the CD in their computer. The melody and lyrics are included in the book so that you can sing or simply follow along.

VOL. 1 – ROCK	00699570 / $14.95	VOL. 40 – INCUBUS	00699668 / $16.95
VOL. 2 – ACOUSTIC	00699569 / $16.95	VOL. 41 – ERIC CLAPTON	00699669 / $16.95
VOL. 3 – HARD ROCK	00699573 / $16.95	VOL. 42 – CHART HITS	00699670 / $16.95
VOL. 4 – POP/ROCK	00699571 / $14.95	VOL. 43 – LYNYRD SKYNYRD	00699681 / $17.95
VOL. 5 – MODERN ROCK	00699574 / $14.95	VOL. 44 – JAZZ	00699689 / $14.95
VOL. 6 – '90s ROCK	00699572 / $14.95	VOL. 45 – TV THEMES	00699718 / $14.95
VOL. 7 – BLUES	00699575 / $16.95	VOL. 46 – MAINSTREAM ROCK	00699722 / $16.95
VOL. 8 – ROCK	00699585 / $14.95	VOL. 47 – HENDRIX SMASH HITS	00699723 / $17.95
VOL. 9 – PUNK ROCK	00699576 / $14.95	VOL. 48 – AEROSMITH CLASSICS	00699724 / $14.95
VOL. 10 – ACOUSTIC	00699586 / $16.95	VOL. 49 – STEVIE RAY VAUGHAN	00699725 / $16.95
VOL. 11 – EARLY ROCK	00699579 / $14.95	VOL. 50 – NÜ METAL	00699726 / $14.95
VOL. 12 – POP/ROCK	00699587 / $14.95	VOL. 51 – ALTERNATIVE '90s	00699727 / $12.95
VOL. 13 – FOLK ROCK	00699581 / $14.95	VOL. 52 – FUNK	00699728 / $12.95
VOL. 14 – BLUES ROCK	00699582 / $16.95	VOL. 54 – HEAVY METAL	00699730 / $14.95
VOL. 15 – R&B	00699583 / $14.95	VOL. 55 – POP METAL	00699731 / $14.95
VOL. 16 – JAZZ	00699584 / $15.95	VOL. 56 – FOO FIGHTERS	00699749 / $14.95
VOL. 17 – COUNTRY	00699588 / $15.95	VOL. 57 – SYSTEM OF A DOWN	00699751 / $14.95
VOL. 18 – ACOUSTIC ROCK	00699577 / $15.95	VOL. 58 – BLINK-182	00699772 / $14.95
VOL. 19 – SOUL	00699578 / $14.95	VOL. 59 – GODSMACK	00699773 / $14.95
VOL. 20 – ROCKABILLY	00699580 / $14.95	VOL. 60 – 3 DOORS DOWN	00699774 / $14.95
VOL. 21 – YULETIDE	00699602 / $14.95	VOL. 61 – SLIPKNOT	00699775 / $14.95
VOL. 22 – CHRISTMAS	00699600 / $14.95	VOL. 62 – CHRISTMAS CAROLS	00699798 / $12.95
VOL. 23 – SURF	00699635 / $14.95	VOL. 63 – CREEDENCE CLEARWATER REVIVAL	00699802 / $14.95
VOL. 24 – ERIC CLAPTON	00699649 / $16.95	VOL. 64 – OZZY OSBOURNE	00699803 / $14.95
VOL. 25 – LENNON & McCARTNEY	00699642 / $14.95	VOL. 65 – THE DOORS	00699806 / $14.95
VOL. 26 – ELVIS PRESLEY	00699643 / $14.95	VOL. 66 – THE ROLLING STONES	00699807 / $16.95
VOL. 27 – DAVID LEE ROTH	00699645 / $16.95	VOL. 67 – BLACK SABBATH	00699808 / $14.95
VOL. 28 – GREG KOCH	00699646 / $14.95	VOL. 68 – PINK FLOYD – DARK SIDE OF THE MOON	00699809 / $14.95
VOL. 29 – BOB SEGER	00699647 / $14.95	VOL. 69 – ACOUSTIC FAVORITES	00699810 / $14.95
VOL. 30 – KISS	00699644 / $14.95	VOL. 74 – PAUL BALOCHE	00699831 / $14.95
VOL. 31 – CHRISTMAS HITS	00699652 / $14.95	VOL. 75 – TOM PETTY	00699882 / $14.95
VOL. 32 – THE OFFSPRING	00699653 / $14.95	VOL. 76 – COUNTRY HITS	00699884 / $12.95
VOL. 33 – ACOUSTIC CLASSICS	00699656 / $16.95	VOL. 78 – NIRVANA	00700132 / $14.9
VOL. 34 – CLASSIC ROCK	00699658 / $16.95		
VOL. 35 – HAIR METAL	00699660 / $16.95		
VOL. 36 – SOUTHERN ROCK	00699661 / $16.95		
VOL. 37 – ACOUSTIC METAL	00699662 / $16.95		
VOL. 38 – BLUES	00699663 / $16.95		
VOL. 39 – '80s METAL	00699664 / $16.95		

Prices, contents, and availability subject to change without notice.

FOR MORE INFORMATION, SEE YOUR LOCAL MUSIC DEALER, OR WRITE TO:

HAL•LEONARD® CORPORATION

7777 W. BLUEMOUND RD. P.O. BOX 13819 MILWAUKEE, WI 532

Visit Hal Leonard online at www.halleon

Complete song lists available online.

Get Better at Guitar

...with these Great Guitar Instruction Books from Hal Leonard!

101 GUITAR TIPS

STUFF ALL THE PROS KNOW AND USE
by Adam St. James
This book contains invaluable guidance on everything from scales and music theory to truss rod adjustments, proper recording studio set-ups, and much more. The book also features snippets of advice from some of the most celebrated guitarists and producers in the music business, including B.B. King, Steve Vai, Joe Satriani, Warren Haynes, Laurence Juber, Pete Anderson, Tom Dowd and others, culled from the author's hundreds of interviews.
00695737 Book/CD Pack..$16.95

AMAZING PHRASING

50 WAYS TO IMPROVE YOUR IMPROVISATIONAL SKILLS
by Tom Kolb
This book/CD pack explores all the main components necessary for crafting well-balanced rhythmic and melodic phrases. It also explains how these phrases are put together to form cohesive solos. Many styles are covered – rock, blues, jazz, fusion, country, Latin, funk and more – and all of the concepts are backed up with musical examples. The companion CD contains 89 demos for listening, and most tracks feature full-band backing.
00695583 Book/CD Pack..$19.95

BLUES YOU CAN USE

by John Ganapes
A comprehensive source designed to help guitarists develop both lead and rhythm playing. Covers: Texas, Delta, R&B, early rock and roll, gospel, blues/rock and more. Includes: 21 complete solos • chord progressions and riffs • turnarounds • moveable scales and more. CD features leads and full band backing.
00695007 Book/CD Pack..$19.95

FRETBOARD MASTERY

by Troy Stetina
Untangle the mysterious regions of the guitar fretboard and unlock your potential. *Fretboard Mastery* familiarizes you with all the shapes you need to know by applying them in real musical examples, thereby ...forcing and reaffirming your ... is a much higher level of
...............$19.95

FRETBOARD ROADMAPS – 2ND EDITION
ESSENTIAL GUITAR PATTERNS THAT ALL THE PROS KNOW AND USE
by Fred Sokolow
The updated edition of this bestseller features more songs, updated lessons, and a full audio CD! Learn to play lead and rhythm anywhere on the fretboard, in any key; play a variety of lead guitar styles; play chords and progressions anywhere on the fretboard; expand your chord vocabulary; and learn to think musically – the way the pros do.
00695941 Book/CD Pack..$14.95

GUITAR AEROBICS

A 52-WEEK, ONE-LICK-PER-DAY WORKOUT PROGRAM FOR DEVELOPING, IMPROVING & MAINTAINING GUITAR TECHNIQUE
by Troy Nelson
From the former editor of *Guitar One* magazine, here is a daily dose of vitamins to keep your chops fine tuned! Musical styles include rock, blues, jazz, metal, country, and funk. Techniques taught include alternate picking, arpeggios, sweep picking, string skipping, legato, string bending, and rhythm guitar. These exercises will increase speed, and improve dexterity and pick- and fret-hand accuracy. The accompanying CD includes all 365 workout licks plus play-along grooves in every style at eight different metronome settings.
00695946 Book/CD Pack..$19.95

GUITAR CLUES

OPERATION PENTATONIC
by Greg Koch
Join renowned guitar master Greg Koch as he clues you in to a wide variety of fun and valuable pentatonic scale applications. Whether you're new to improvising or have been doing it for a while, this book/CD pack will provide loads of delicious licks and tricks that you can use right away, from volume swells and chicken pickin' to intervallic and chordal ideas. The CD includes 65 demo and play-along tracks.
00695827 Book/CD Pack..$19.95

INTRODUCTION TO GUITAR TONE & EFFECTS
by David M. Brewster
This book/CD pack teaches the basics of guitar tones and effects, with audio examples on CD. Readers will learn about: overdrive, distortion and fuzz • using equalizers • modulation effects • reverb and delay • multi-effect processors • and more.
00695766 Book/CD Pack..$14.95

PICTURE CHORD ENCYCLOPEDIA
This comprehensive guitar chord resource for all playing styles and levels features five voicings of 44 chord qualities for all twelve keys – 2,640 chords in all! For each, there is a clearly illustrated chord frame, as well as *an actual photo* of the chord being played! Includes info on basic fingering principles, open chords and barre chords, partial chords and broken-set forms, and more.
00695224 ....$19.95

SCALE CHORD RELATIONSHIPS

by Michael Mueller & Jeff Schroedl
This book teaches players how to determine which scales to play with which chords, so guitarists will never have to fear chord changes again! This book/CD pack explains how to: recognize keys • analyze chord progressions • use the modes • play over nondiatonic harmony • use harmonic and melodic minor scales • use symmetrical scales such as chromatic, whole-tone and diminished scales • incorporate exotic scales such as Hungarian major and Gypsy minor • and much more!
00695563 Book/CD Pack..$14.95

SPEED MECHANICS FOR LEAD GUITAR
Take your playing to the stratosphere with the most advanced lead book by this proven heavy metal author. *Speed Mechanics* is the ultimate technique book for developing the kind of speed and precision in today's explosive playing styles. Learn the fastest ways to achieve speed and control, secrets to make your practice time really count, and how to open your ears and make your musical ideas more solid and tangible. Packed with over 200 vicious exercises including Troy's scorching version of "Flight of the Bumblebee." Music and examples demonstrated on CD. 89-minute audio.
00699323 Book/CD Pack..$19.95

TOTAL ROCK GUITAR
A COMPLETE GUIDE TO LEARNING ROCK GUITAR
by Troy Stetina
This unique and comprehensive source for learning rock guitar is designed to develop both lead and rhythm playing. It covers: getting a tone that rocks • open chords, power chords and barre chords • riffs, scales and licks • string bending, strumming, palm muting, harmonics and alternate picking • all rock styles • and much more. The examples are in standard notation with chord grids and tab, and the CD includes full-band backing for all 22 songs.
00695246 Book/CD Pack..$17.95

0308